AN ESSAY

ON THE

ECONOMIC CAUSES OF FAMINES IN INDIA

AN ESSAY

ON THE

ECONOMIC CAUSES OF FAMINES IN INDIA

AND

Suggestions to prevent their frequent recurrence.

BEING THE

Biresvar mitter prize Essap for 1905.

SATISCHANDRA RAY, M. A.

GYAN

Published by

GYAN

Gyan Publishing House
5, Ansari Road
Daryaganj, New Delhi-110002
Phone: 011-47034999, 9811692060
E-mail: books@gyanbooks.com

Distribution Network
gyanbooks.com
India, USA, Canada, UK, Australia, France

ISBN: 978-81-212-9374-7 (PB)
First Published, 1909

2nd Impression 2023

Printed at: Gyan Press, Delhi.

AN ESSAY ON THE ECONOMIC CAUSES OF FAMINES IN INDIA

AUTHOR: SATISCHANDRA RAY

AN ESSAY

ON THE

Economic Causes of Famines in India

AND

Suggestions to prevent their frequent recurrence.

BEING THE

Biresvar Mitter Prize Essay for 1905.

BY

SATISCHANDRA RAY, M.A.

Calcutta:

PUBLISHED BY THE CALCUTTA UNIVERSITY AND PRINTED AT THE BAPTIST MISSION PRESS.

1909.

An Essay on the Economic Causes of Famines in India and Suggestions to prevent their Frequent Recurrence.

Preliminary.

There is no subject so important, so far-reaching, and, at the same time, so controversial in the domain of Indian administration and economics as the subject of famines. In India famine has, perhaps, played a more momentous—rather a more tragic—part in the history of the Empire than either a great war, a great revolution, or a great pestilence. The controversial character of the subject arises from the fact that different schools of thought and action attribute the causes of famine to different circumstances, and suggest widely different remedies for its prevention, or for the mitigation of its desolating consequences. These causes may be broadly classified under two heads : (1) Physical, (2) Economic. There is obviously no connection between the physical and the economic causes, but it is beyond dispute that the former are aggravated by the latter. Although, therefore, the subject of this essay is the investigation into the economic causes of famines, I am unable to dismiss altogether from consideration all references to physical causes which are directly responsible for the vicissitudes of season, bringing with them, in their train, failure of crops and scarcity. We have practically no scientific knowledge of the physical causes of rainfall, and the regulation of the atmospheric aberrations is beyond human control. Assuming, therefore, that the periodicity of rainfall is uncertain and capricious, and that there is no control over either the beneficent or the destructive forces of nature, we must accept the physical causes and their consequences as inevitable, and consider only those which are within the range of human foresight and control.

Causes :—physical and economic.

History of famines.

The subject cannot be adequately and comprehensively dealt with without prefacing it with a brief history of famines in the past. During the ninety years of administration by the East India

Company, there occurred twelve famines and four severe scarcities; and during the fifty years that followed the assumption of the Empire by the Crown, there have been ten famines and two severe scarcities. Before 1868, famine relief was administered on no systematic principles, and the policy of the Government was dictated by the circumstances of the occasion. The statistics compiled by the Famine Commission of 1880 in regard to famines that occurred before 1868, are not so reliable as to lead to correct and satisfactory conclusions. The first change in the principles and practice of famine relief was inaugurated after the famine of 1868 in Northern India; and it was not till the Report of the Commission of 1880 was issued, that the terrible famine of 1876-78 forced upon the Government of India the necessity of laying down definite and authoritative principles for a clear recognition of state responsibility, for the systematic administration of famines with the aid of codes suitable to the circumstances of each province, and for a radical change in the financial policy. It would be beyond the scope and limits of this essay to go back to the history of famines prior to 1876-78, when the first important advance in the famine policy of the Government was made. But it would be necessary for a proper comprehension of the subject to narrate the general effects of the famines which have since affected different parts of the continent.

Famine relief policy.

The famine of 1876-78 is thus described by the Famine Commissioners of 1880: "The great famine in Southern India, which has so recently come to an end, has been, in respect of the area and population affected, and the duration and intensity of the distress, the most grievous calamity of its kind experienced in British India since the beginning of the century. . . . The total area which suffered from famine in Southern India during 1877 was about 200,000 square miles, with a population of 36 millions. In the next year, an area of 52,000 square miles in the North-Western Provinces and the Punjab, with a population of 22 millions, was affected by a failure of the rains, though it suffered to a far less degree. Distinguishing the three degrees of famine as intense, severe and slight, the famine in Southern India was intense in an area of 105,000 square miles inhabited by a population of 19 millions; it was severe in an area of 66,000 square miles, with a population of 11 millions; and it was slight in an area of 34,000 square miles, with a population of 6 millions. Where the distress was but slight the necessity for giving relief arose only in isolated localities, and the administration of famine relief on such a scale as to need special

Famine of 1876-78.

measures was in practice confined to the tracts where the famine was intense or severe. Relief was afforded to 780,000 persons, or 5 per cent. of the population of the more afflicted area in Madras for 22 consecutive months; and in Bombay, to 320,000 persons, or $3\frac{1}{2}$ per cent., for 13 months. The maximum number relieved during the worst month was about 500,000, daily in Bombay, and $2\frac{1}{4}$ millions in Madras, or, from 6 to 15 per cent. of the population severely afflicted." It has been officially estimated that the mortality that occurred during the famine of 1876-78 amounted to $5\frac{1}{2}$ millions in excess of the normal rate. The number of births, which generally receive a check during a period of starvation and distress was, it is estimated, reduced by two millions. The total reduction of population, by death and by loss of fecundity, is accordingly computed at 7 millions. After a careful consideration of the relation that subsists between famine mortality and normal mortality, the Famine Commissioners of 1880 came to the conclusion that, the population of India is perpetually exposed to destructive agencies, which, under more favourable conditions, might be regarded as preventible; but against which, they remarked, society, at its present stage of education and knowledge, is unable to protect itself. Famine, they continued, intensifies the activity of these periodical epidemics; but it is not the only one of the numerous influences by which human life is cut short. They, therefore, concluded that human endeavours are powerless to prevent an increase of mortality during a severe famine. For these reasons it is not practicable to discriminate with precision, between the mortality due directly to starvation and that due to diseases brought on by starvation. Nevertheless, it cannot be denied that there is a close connection between famine and the abnormal mortality which follows; and it would not be far from the truth to attribute the total mortality during a famine, after deducting the normal rate, as arising directly or indirectly from that terrible cause.

Mortality.

The total expenditure on the famine of 1876-78 was about 8 crores of rupees, and the total loss of revenue about 3 crores. The net financial effect of this dire calamity was, therefore, about 11 crores of rupees.

Conclusions as to future famines.

The conclusions drawn by the Famine Commissioners from the foregoing statistics are that no case occurred in the history of the past which has surpassed the famine of 1876-78 in intensity; and it seemed to them reasonable to arrive at the conclusion that it was not likely to be exceeded in future either in extent or the degree of relief that would be necessary. Relying on this presumption they predicted that "the largest population likely to be severely affected by famine at one time may be put at 30 millions. To arrive at the numbers likely to come on relief we may safely take a proportion slightly lower than that of the Bihar famine, say, 15 per cent., or 4½ millions, as the maximum number likely to be in receipt of relief in the worst months, and about 7 or 8 per cent., or from 2 to 2½ millions as the average number likely to require relief continuously for the space of a year. These proportions provide for a scale about double that actually given in Madras and Bombay in 1876-78." Until 1896-97 it was officially believed that these predictions had stood the test of experience of the past, and that there was no reason to deviate from these conclusions in estimating the financial and administrative resources of the Government during the most intense famines. I shall, however, show later on how these predictions have been falsified in the subsequent history of Indian famines.

Recent famines.

Between the year of the publication of the Report of the Famine Commission and the present time, famines of more or less intensity have occurred in different parts of the continent out of which the following deserve to be chronicled :—

(i) The Bihar and Madras Famine of 1888-89.
(ii) Famine of 1891-92.
(iii) Famine of 1896-97.
(iv) Famine of 1899-1900.
(v) Famine of 1906-1907.
(vi) Famine of 1907-1908.

Famine of 1888-89.

The Bihar and Madras Famine of 1888-89 affected an area of 3,500 square miles, containing a population of little over a million people. The maximum daily number employed on relief works was about 64,000, and that in receipt of gratuitous relief, 110,000. The total cost, including remissions and suspensions of land revenue, and loans and advances, was about 25½ lakhs of rupees. There are no reliable statistics of mortality.

Famine of 1891-92.

The famine of 1891-92 affected an area of 50,000 square miles, inhabited by a population exceeding 7 millions. The maximum daily number employed on relief works was 240,000 ; and, the total cost, including special establishment charges, loans, remissions of revenue, &c., exceeded a crore of rupees.

The famine of 1896-97 was more wide-spread and severe than any of its predecessors, and it has been officially described as the most disastrous famine of the century. The total affected area in British territory was about 225,000 square miles, containing a population of 62 millions of souls. The number of persons in receipt of relief grew from 50,000 in October, 1896, to 3,300,000 in April, 1897. Of the latter, about 2½ millions were employed on relief works, and the remainder were in receipt of gratuitous relief. The percentage of average daily number relieved to the total population varied from 5·3 in Bengal to 14·8 in the United Provinces. In Madras it was 12·9, in the Central Provinces it was 10·3, in Bombay 12·1, and in the Punjab 9·3 in the most severely smitten tracts. At the end of September the total number fell to 1,344,000 persons, namely, 646,000 on works, and 698,000 on gratuitous relief. The aggregate number of units relieved from October, 1896, to September, 1897, amounted to the colossal figure of 800 millions. There are no reliable statistics of mortality attending this famine from which conclusions can be drawn; but as stated by Mr. Holderness in his Narrative of Famine [Parliamentary Paper Cd. 8812 of 1897] the materials are "unfortunately sufficient for the conclusion that a considerable excess of mortality rate has attended the late famine. The relation of the mortality in India to famine was carefully considered in 1881 by the Famine Commission, and their remarks are apposite to the present occasion."

Famine of 1896-97.

The cost is represented by the following figures:

Actual expenditure in 1896-97	..	2,06 lakhs
,, ,, 1897-98	..	5,32 ,,
Loss of revenue in the two years	..	6,40 ,,
Indirect expenditure ..	..	2,00 ,,
Loans and advances ..	..	1,29 ,,
Total		17,07 lakhs

In other words, the finances of the Government of India were strained to the extent of 17 crores of rupees in consequence of this disastrous calamity. In addition to this enormous expenditure of Government funds, a sum of 1½ crores of rupees was expended out of the Indian Famine Charitable Relief Fund raised by public subscriptions.

The famine of 1899-1900 occurred before the ravages done by its predecessor had been completely effaced or forgotten. The people had

Famine of 1899-1900.

hardly recovered from the terrible visitations of 1896-97, the country had not had sufficient time for recuperation, Nature had yet hardly clothed the parched-up tracts with green vegetation, the thirst of the dried-up tanks and wells had not yet been fully quenched, the strain on the financial and administrative resources of the Government had not yet been fully relaxed—when another famine, hardly less severe, visited an area of 189,000 square miles of British territory inhabited by a population of 28 millions. "The circumstances of the famine of 1899-1900," according to Sir A. Macdonnell's Report of 1901, "are in many ways peculiar. Both in its material manifestations and in the attitude of the people it differs from preceding famines. . . . Shortness of the water-supply, and dearth of fodder told heavily on men and cattle and enormously increased the difficulties of administration. Moreover, in the districts bordering on Native States, immigration added very greatly to the anxieties of the local officers; . . . but the most distinctive feature of the recent famine, from the administrative point of view, was the number of persons who came on State relief. These far exceeded the numbers of any previous famine." Compared with the famine of 1896-97 the population of the affected area was greater by 61 per cent. in the Central Provinces; 145 per cent. in Berar, and 42 per cent. in Bombay. The number of units relieved was higher by 252 per cent. in the Central Provinces, 2,040 per cent. in Berar; 224 per cent. in Bombay; and 119 per cent. in the Punjab. The total number of persons in receipt of relief in October, 1899, when the first warnings of the impending calamity were sounded, was 688,000, which reached the maximum of 4,600,000 in July, 1900, when the famine assumed its worst features. From July to November, the number steadily diminished, until on the 24th of November it dwindled down to 229,000. "The Famine Commission of 1880," continues the Report, "estimated that 15 per cent. of the population affected was the maximum number likely to be in receipt of relief in the worst months ; and that about 7 or 8 per cent. was the average number likely to require relief continuously for the space of a year. The Commission of 1898 pointed out that these proportions had been largely exceeded in certain areas in 1897. But a much greater excess had been recorded, over larger areas, and for longer periods, in the recent famine, particularly in the Central Provinces." The minimum and maximum percentages for five provinces are noted below :—

	Min.	Max
Central Provinces ..	14·50	22·28
Berar	6·5	15·7
Bombay	5·25	16·4
Ajmer	10·1	26·6
Punjab	2·4	13·20

An examination of these statistics clearly indicates that these high figures are due to either of two causes, or to a combination of both : (*a*) leniency in the administration of famine relief; (*b*) economic exhaustion of the people in consequence of the preceding famine. In regard to the latter, the Governor-General stated in the Legislative Council on the 19th Oct. 1900 that " on a very cautious estimate, the production in 1899-1900 must have been at least one-quarter, if not one-third, below the average. At normal prices, the loss was at least 75 crores or 50 millions sterling. In this estimate, India is treated as a whole. But in reality the loss fell on a portion only of the continent.....If to this be added the value of some millions of cattle, some conception may be formed of the destruction of property which a great drought occasions. There have been many great droughts in India; but there has been no other of which such figures could be predicated as these." This harrowing account painfully strikes the imagination with a gloomy picture of the severe economic strain to which the people are subjected in times of famine. And it is obvious that the physical conditions which induced the famine of 1899-1900 were greatly influenced and accentuated by the economic causes which had left their traces since 1896.

The cost of relief measures connected with this famine was :—

Direct expenditure in 1899-1900 ..	3,11	lakhs.
Ditto in 1900-01 ..	6,18	,,
Loss of revenue in the two years ..	3,52	,,
Indirect expenditure	1,30	,,
Loans, etc.	2,40	,,
TOTAL ..	16,51	lakhs.

The net financial effect on the revenues of the Government of India was, therefore, more than 16½ crores of rupees.

Mortality during 1891-1901.

The mortality which had occurred during the 10 years 1891-1901, can be ascertained with some approximation to correctness from the Census Reports. The Provinces which were most affected by the famine during this decennial period are,

Bombay, the United Provinces, the Central Provinces, Central India, Rajputana, Ajmer and Berar. The total population of these provinces returned by the Census Report of 1891 was 113,350,000 (including the Native States) as contrasted with 107,420,000 returned by the Census of 1901. Assuming the normal rate of increase in a decennial period to be 6 per cent. on the most cautious assumption, the population in 1901 should have naturally grown to 120,150,000. The actual facts, on the contrary, disclose that the population has fallen off by 12¾ millions. This deficiency represents the mortality due to famines, to plague, to diseases incidental to famine, to emigration* and to other causes. Most of these causes are at work in normal times, and the deficiency may justifiably be attributed to starvation and diseases brought on by starvation. It is contended that diminished fecundity, emigration, intensification of the normal causes by famine conditions, etc., account for a substantial share of the mortality. But even on the most optimistic supposition, and making allowance for all ordinary causes, the mortality during the 10 years arising directly and indirectly from starvation and distress cannot be put at a lower figure than 10 millions.

The statistics of the famines of 1906-7 and 1907-8 are not yet fully available.

Conclusions as to cost of famines.

The statistics of the two calamitous famines of 1896-97 and 1899-1900 unmistakably show that the estimate of the Famine Commissioners of 1880 in regard to the maximum number likely to claim State charity in future famines has been, unhappily, falsified. The number of people likely to be affected by famine and to demand relief, cannot be regulated by any hard and fast principle or by any rule of averages. The Commissioners stated in para. 100 of their Report that "taking the figures before arrived at as indicating the probable maximum number of persons to be relieved in the worst famine for an average time of one year to be 2½ millions, and reckoning the cost per head, including all contingencies, as not likely to exceed 50 rupees, the maximum charge in any future year would be 12½ millions sterling (or 12½ crores of rupees). But such extreme cases would be of rare occurrence, and the average numbers for a series of years would be far less, not amounting to more than 250,000 yearly." Recent experience has shown, beyond the shadow of doubt, that these numbers, far less the extent and severity of a famine, cannot be regulated by human calculations or reduced to mathe-

* The plague and emigration statistics of the 10 years show that the population was reduced by 660,000 from these two causes. They therefore affect the total mortality to an inconsiderable extent.

matical formulæ. Given certain aggravating circumstances, it is quite conceivable that even the "improbable" estimate of the Famine Commissioners may, at times, be reached, or even exceeded. This is not a very extravagant theory, and the wisdom of man can be no guarantee against its realisation.

From a brief historical narrative of the most important of the famines that occurred during the preceding 30 years, I pass on to examine the causes that produced them. It would be convenient if, in this investigation, the remedies were considered side by side with the causes.

Economic causes—Poverty and indebtedness.

The most vital economic causes from which distress and starvation generally originate during a period of drought are the want of resourcefulness or resisting capacity of the ryots, their chronic poverty, their indebtedness, and generally their improvident habits. Such a fierce controversy has raged round this subject that it would be prudent to avoid all dry and monotonous statistics of calculations and all controversial points and to discuss the question on broad and general principles, based on facts or authoritative statements. The impoverished condition of the Indian peasant is proverbial and has never been disputed by the highest authorities either in this country or in England. Lord George Hamilton, speaking before the House of Commons on February 3, 1902, said: "I agree at once that India is very poor. I admit that one section of the agricultural community are becoming more and more in debt." Again, on November 10, following, he stated: "I admit readily that India is a very poor country and there are dense masses of poverty located there, and that the partition between the ordinary wage of the coolie and indigence is very thin, and their general standard of life and comfort is far below that of European nations." Similar views of India's poverty have been expressed by Lord Curzon in the Legislative Council and by the Right Honourable Mr. Brodrick (now Lord Midleton) in the House of Commons on August 12, 1904. In spite of this poverty, the people are able to maintain themselves, because food is 'extraordinarily cheap,' and the climatic conditions limit their necessaries of life to so low a standard that they can afford to live on £2 or 30 rupees a year. There are no published statistics bearing on the economic condition of the agriculturist, and whatever exist in published form are either too fragmentary or untrustworthy to be utilised for a scientific investigation of the subject. It is not, therefore, possible to make a satisfactory inquiry into the condition of the people; and in these circumstances, I am constrained to accept the general statements made, and the conclusions arrived at, by responsible authorities, *viz.*, that the people of India are poor and that they are too improvident and resourceless to protect themselves against the physical and economic effects of calamitous seasons.

The circumstance that, at the first warning of an impending famine, millions of people flock to the relief works where they receive a daily subsistence wage of 5 or 6 pice can only be explained on one of two hypotheses: (*a*) that no food is available in the country; (*b*) that the people are devoid of any accumulated saving, represented by the sum of 20 or 30 rupees, by means of which they can purchase a livelihood during a stress of 7 or 8 months. The first of these hypotheses has no foundation on facts. Lord George Hamilton stated on February 3, 1902: "What does drought mean? It is not a question of food; the scarcity of food in a district affected by drought is the least of the evils with which the Government of India have to deal. There is nearly always a sufficiency of food in India to feed all the people within its limits; and, owing to the development of the railway, the British Government are able, no matter what part of the country may be affected, to pour in sufficient food to maintain the people of the district." The Famine Commissioners of 1898, who made an exhaustive inquiry into the question, came to the conclusion that "the surplus produce of India, taken as a whole, still furnished ample means of meeting the demands of any part of the country likely to suffer from famine at one time, supposing such famine to be not greater in extent and duration than hitherto experienced. If proof is wanted, it is found in the fact that during the late (1896-97) famine . . the stocks at the end do not seem to have been close on exhaustion, though the only import from outside was some 600,000 tons from Burma. No doubt the high prices led to great, and often painful, economy of consumption, but, nevertheless, the result indicates considerable ordinary surplus and accumulated stocks." These views had been independently stated by the late General Sir R. Strachey, in a speech before the Royal Institution of Great Britain, on May 18, 1877, in which he confidently declared that taking the country as a whole "the food-supply easily provides for the entire population under all known circumstances, and that in the late severe Bengal famine, the export of grain continued without very great diminution in spite of the failure of crops." These conclusions dispel the popular theory that there is no sufficient food available in the country to feed a starving population, and lead us, naturally, to the second of the two hypotheses stated above, namely, that the people are too poor to buy the food which already exists in the country.

Now, what is the extent of the resources necessary to enable a famine-stricken people to weather a period of, say, 8 months of distress and starvation ? Here again I must rely on the official statement made by the Secretary of State for India, who said on February 3, 1902 : "I was looking through some papers the other day, which were prepared in Lord Dufferin's time, and I came across a statement which I believe to be absolutely true as to what a man can do on an income of Rs. 6 a month. That is 96 pence, and it gives a man a little more than 3 pence a day. Anyone in receipt of this 3 pence a day and being the head of a family, consisting of not more than four, could give his family every day three meals of rice or millet, and fish, if near the coast, and butcher's meat once or twice a week ; but there would be no milk, or butter, or cheese for the children." Allowing for an increase in the price of food during a scarcity, and for the sacrifice of some meals a month, as well as for general economy of consumption, it may be inferred that Rs. 30 or 40 in all, would suffice to maintain an individual and his family during the worst months of famine. And it follows as a corollary that want of this insignificant capital, either in the shape of cash or ornaments or other articles of marketable value, drives an agricultural labourer and his family to the horrors and privations of famine camps. In other words, distress and starvation are the result of a lack of resources represented by six months' wages of a relief camp labourer. When it is remembered that famines recur at the end of each quinquennium it is impossible to resist the conclusion that the earning member of a rural family is unable to save, in normal seasons, Rs. 40 in five years, or Rs. 8 a year, as an insurance against death by starvation.

An attempt is commonly made to controvert this fact by referring to the increase in the Savings Bank deposits as an unfailing indication of the growing material prosperity of the *people*, by which we are to understand, in Lord Curzon's words, "the patient, humble millions toiling at the well and at the plough, knowing little of budgets (and, I would add, of Savings Banks) but very painfully aware of the narrow margin between sufficiency and indigence." A little reflection will convince the reader that this assertion is incompatible with the conclusions arrived at above. Indeed, there is not the slightest connection between the deposits in Savings Banks, to which the agriculturists rarely resort, and improvement in their material condition ; for, if there had been any such connection, they would have instantly fallen back on the reserve instead of having allowed themselves, and their dear ones, to die of hunger and diseases induced by starvation In making the assertion it is generally forgotten that there exists in India a lower stratum of the population than that which contributes to the unfunded balance of the Government. This stratum is represented by the starving peasantry which constitute nearly 68 per cent. of the total population of British India, who hardly use any imported articles except a few yards of cotton stuff, or a few bottles of oil, and who are ignorant, I may say, of even the existence of Savings Banks in this country. The number of depositors in the Post Office Savings Banks—and, for obvious reasons, I leave the other banks out of account—barely exceed one million people. What is one million out of 295 millions of the total, and 198 millions of the agricultural and labouring, population of India? It sounds extraordinary to assert that the material condition of 294 millions can be precisely judged by the condition of the one million of Savings Bank depositors. Indeed, in the Post Office Savings Banks, agriculture plays but an insignificant part, represented by only about 17,000 depositors, other professions and industries enjoying the preponderating share.

The cause of this poverty, in its chronic and epidemic form, is believed to be the improvident habits of the ryot which drive him to indebtedness. Referring to this indebtedness, the Famine Commissioners of 1901 write: "We desire to call special attention to the agrarian system introduced by the survey settlement as an accentuating cause of indebtedness, and more specially to the unrestricted right of the cultivators to transfer their holdings which the survey settlement recognised. . . . A leading principle of the revenue system, as finally established, was that, in view of the moderation of assessment, sufficient elasticity was given by making the assessment of each 'field' separate, and by giving the registered occupant complete power of transfer or relinquishment over his 'field.' A strong tenure of this sort, held at a low assessment, was a very valuable property; and, it is easy to see now that it would have been wise to have kept a vigilant watch over the use which an ignorant and unthrifty peasantry was making of it. . . . It was decided that there should be no interference by Government with the people and that no inquiries should be made regarding the financial condition of the cultivators. Thus, things were left to take their own course; and the result was—as invariably happens when an ignorant and improvident peasantry can dispose, without restriction, of valuable rights in land—that cultivators sank deeper into debt, and their property began to pass out of their hands. It must be admitted that the conditions, on which, under the revenue system, the cultivators held their lands, helped to bring this result about: the rigidity of the revenue system forced them into debt, while the valuable property which they held made it easy to borrow." Lord George Hamilton puts the same view in different language as follows: "If we had so taxed the agriculturist that he could not get a livelihood out of his holding, the money-lender would not advance large sums of money on a security that was of little value. It is to the fact that we have given this asset of great value to the agriculturist, and to the fact that we have also, by the alterations we have effected in the law, given the money-lender facilities that he had never before, and security which he never had before, that we must attribute this great increase in indebtedness. I have, on more than one occasion, in this House, ventured to express my opinion that, as regards the future of India, the most serious difficulties that this country can have to encounter are not inherited with the system of native Government which we took over, or are inherent in that system, but they are of our own creation." The striking note in the two official pronouncements quoted above is that lands in this country are assessed very low. There is much difference of opinion on this point. But there is one point that has been obscured in the discussion. The money-lender does not value the lands as an asset of great value because the assessment is low. According to the law which governs all human nature, every man desires to possess what he has not. A landless money-lender hankers after land in the same way as a moneyless landlord hankers after money. Money-lending business having no charms for the man any longer, he seeks after new methods of investment and places his faith in land as being a far less fluid asset than ready cash. He begins to lend money to cultivators, among whom a demand for borrowing is very brisk, on the security of their only asset, the land. The money-lender is certain that the land will ultimately fall into his grasp, and that his hopes of becoming a landholder will be ultimately realised. The inducement to lend money to the cultivators is, in my opinion, not the low assessment, but the hope of becoming a landed proprietor—respected of the people and possessing a status in the community. The argument that an unrestricted right of transferring a valuable property leads the owner to borrowing propensities and precipitates his ruin is at once weak and far-fetched. Every owner of property possesses unrestricted right of alienation; but every such person is not a borrower. It would be more natural to argue that the desire in a man for borrowing is induced by poverty—by desperate poverty—when he has no other resources to fall back upon than the valuable property which is the mainstay of support of himself and his family. It is indisputable that the cultivator has no better financial reserve than the land he holds, and that he is driven in necessitous times to borrow on the security of his only property of value. The most peremptory necessity for borrowing arises when the demand for Government revenue comes to be enforced; and it is at that supreme moment that he places all his resources at the feet of the Collector—sacrificing health and comfort and the last ray of hope and cheerfulness.

Government measures against increase of rural indebtedness.

The Government have lately recognised the gravity of rural indebtedness and have inaugurated two measures to remedy the situation. The one is to prevent the easy alienation of the ryot's holding, and the other, to make him independent of the usurious creditor. An instalment of the first measure was introduced into the Punjab, but it was stoutly opposed as revolutionary by a certain section of the Indian and the European community. In enacting the Alienation of Land Act, the Government was actuated by the highest and most beneficent motive, and unless experience condemns the measure as a failure, it is too early yet to fully gauge its effects. It is a fundamental law of nature that a spirit of thriftiness is inconsistent with facility for borrowing; and the most effectual way to protect a poor and ignorant ryot from borrowing on the security of his holding is to put an artificial restraint on his power of alienation. The immediate effect of this restriction is expected to be an inducement to economy, the continued practice of which, even under an artificial process, will gradually educate him in the art of permanent thrift. It is too early to condemn the measure on the imaginary ground that it will have the certain effect of depreciating the price of a valuable property. The principle of the measure, it should not be forgotten, is to retain, as far as possible, the holdings, which are the mainstay of the ryots, in their hands; and so long as their livelihood is assured, although at some sacrifice of little luxuries and comforts, it is perfectly immaterial whether his credit is depreciated, rises, or remains stationary. The recent reports on the working of the Act show beyond doubt, that there has been a general tendency to reduce expenses connected with social and religious ceremonies in the Punjab, and that the credit of the agriculturists has been markedly contracted. The practical results so far achieved justify the hope that the measure is fraught with incalculable advantages to those for whom it was designed. We must patiently watch how the provisions of the Act operate, and refrain from expressing an adverse opinion on a measure not induced by any sinister motive which has been adopted on the recommendation of experts.

It is understood that the Punjab Act will serve as a model "for other provinces where the expropriation of the peasantry by the money-lender is a social and political danger." It is hoped that when the time comes for introducing it into the other provinces, the public will gladly welcome it in the interests of the *sowcar*-ridden peasantry.

The second measure of importance which has been adopted by the Government of India to prevent rural indebtedness and bankruptcy is the Co-operative Credit Societies Act. Since the Act was passed people have evinced very little enthusiasm and co-operation in establishing these societies on a firm workable basis. The public mind is naturally growing sceptic about the success of a measure which is a pure imitation of a system prevailing in highly developed communities. The authors of the system have not correctly appreciated the habits and conditions of the rural population as well as the co-operative instincts of the peoples of the land of origin and of the land of adoption. The scheme has, however, much to recommend it. If it takes a firm root in the country it will be fraught with untold benefits to the community. Every facility has been afforded to make it a success: legislation has wisely provided for liberal state support, for simplicity of procedure, and for substantial concessions to the co-operators; but the greatest impediment to success is the ignorance and conservatism of the people. It is impolitic to prophesy, but judging from the experience of the past few years, it will not be rash to infer that, compared with the advantages the system is designed to secure, the enthusiasm in its favour has been somewhat lukewarm, and if it is to be made a success, more encouragement, a more extensive education, and a closer touch and sympathy with the people are necessary. If a paternal Government were seriously minded to raise its subjects from a dead level of ignorance and superstition, the spirit of proud isolation which dominates the officers who are directly responsible for the introduction of reform should be speedily shaken off. The relation between the poor and ignorant learners and the enlightened instructors and reformers must be one of intimate and direct contact like the pupil and the teacher. The former should be freely afforded opportunities to learn the lessons imparted by the latter; but if the people have any cause to doubt the character of the mission of the reformers who work in their midst, the lessons will have been given in vain.

Causes of rural indebtedness.

Rural indebtedness arises from either of two causes: (*a*) inadequacy of the income to secure the bare necessaries of life; (*b*) difficulty to restrict, within means, expenses other than the cost of sustenance. I assume, on official authority, that the income is sufficient not only for bare sustenance, but even for petty luxuries. It therefore follows that the second cause is the only operative cause. Now, the extraordinary expenses of a ryot consist of : (*i*) payment of land revenue demand ; (*ii*) expenditure on ceremonial functions. Great restriction has been placed upon the second class of expenditure by legislative measures in the Punjab and Bombay, and palliative measures have been adopted by the enactment of the Co-operative Credit Societies Act. It will therefore be observed that the principal cause by which the physical effects of dearth are aggravated has been provided for by special legislative measures, and if they prove successful, they will have solved one of the most vital problems affecting agrarian economics.

It now remains to discuss the first point, *viz.*, whether any relief can be provided in the payment of the land revenue demand with reference to which every proposal bearing on reduction or permanence of assessment has been rejected either as unnecessary or inexpedient. No one will venture to throw out the suggestion that the Government of India should forego a substantial portion of the existing land revenue demand of 30 crores of rupees in favour of the ryots with a view to improve their economic condition. This is an idea which is not justifiable on economic principles. A relinquishment of revenue in their favour will not make the ignorant, educated, or the improvident, thrifty. On the contrary, according to the fundamental laws of human nature, the unexpected acquisition of fortune or other valuable concessions will react prejudicially on the industry or thriftiness of the recipient. This will operate as a stimulus to extravagance, and the ryot will sink more and more deeply into poverty and indebtedness. Just as a child needs the fostering care, and the gentle, though firm, treatment, of his parents to make him grow into a perfect type of manhood, the ignorant subjects of India, similarly, need the paternal care and solicitude of Government to convert them into an intelligent, thrifty and industrious population. The Government must proceed slowly, cautiously, and at the same time sympathetically, in the matter. They must avoid all measures of complex administration, the technical and expensive law courts, the innumerable facilities for litigation, and the introduction, generally, of Western models in every branch of administration. These complex and expensive machineries tend directly or indirectly to the pauperisation of the masses, whose ideas of government, of civilisation, of material comfort, of protection against oppression and abuse of law and justice are far behind the times.

The most effective remedial measure which I venture to suggest for affording relief in respect of the payment of land revenue is the extension of the Permanent Settlement.

Permanent Settlement a remedy against famine.

The beneficial influence of no other measure will permeate so thoroughly the masses who possess an interest in the land. The advantages that are likely to accrue to them have been demonstrated by eminent Indian administrators, extracts from whose minutes are given in Appendix A. They argue that the introduction of the Permanent Settlement will stimulate industry and thrift, call forth the latent energies of the people, enable capital to be accumulated in their hands, encourage investment of capital in the improvement of land, increase agricultural wealth, strengthen the social community, and will ultimately compensate the State for the relinquishment of any prospective land revenue by giving the agriculturists greater capacity to purchase taxable articles and by reducing the expenses of periodical assessments. Between the two alternatives, namely, the relinquishment of prospective revenue and the promotion of the well-being of the famine-stricken and impoverished peasantry who constitute the backbone of agricultural India, the choice can never be doubtful nor difficult. The highest and noblest duty is to raise the mass of the population from the dead level to which it has sunk by years of starvation and servitude; and the growth of the material and moral prosperity of the country must attend the improvement of the condition of the preponderating proportion of its population. To adopt legislative remedies for the prevention of indebtedness and the promotion of thrift among the poor and the extravagant, and, at the same time to leave them a bare margin of subsistence, does not touch the fringe of the problem. The ultimate motive in denying the advantages of the Permanent Settlement to the country is the undue apprehension of a loss of revenue. But what useful object, one is inclined to ask, will the mere inflation of the public purse serve, if the person who contributes to it cannot afford to do so except at a great self-denial and without taxing his available resources, and consequently his capacity, to meet the future demands? The interests of the State are ultimately identical with the interests of its subjects; it would, therefore, be unwise if it were to starve the people, after the fashion of the proverbial fool who killed the goose that laid golden eggs, for appropriating the benefits that would ultimately come to it through the people. In view of the large beneficial measures that have been passed from time to time, the motive of the Government in its persistent refusal to introduce the Permanent Settlement generally into India, appears to be somewhat inexplicable.

No one can conscientiously refrain from appreciating the value of the generous financial concessions, in addition to the almost unlimited financial responsibility which the State undertakes during a famine. But these temporary concessions, made to tide over periods of temporary stress, do not, in any way, make for a permanent amelioration of the condition of the people to whom they are granted. Direct pecuniary aids are more demoralising in their character, and more extravagant in effect, than permanent indirect concession in the shape of a fixity of the land revenue demand. Indirect aid has the advantage of elevating the character of a people, of stimulating their energies, of promoting self-help and thrift, and of generally exercising a permanent moral influence over the whole career of their life. Direct aid is merely improvised for the occasion, and its moral and material effects, which are merely evanescent, pass away with the exigencies of the hour. In this view of the case, the Permanent Settlement will exercise a more permanent effect on the habits and character of the people than temporary grants of money, or other direct pecuniary concessions, however valuable or liberal in themselves. The latter, received in times of distress and suffering are, no doubt, most highly appreciated; but they afford only a momentary relief or enjoyment; while the former, coming to them in peaceful and normal times, can be utilised with the most satisfactory practical results.

It has been argued that the increasing cost of administration, necessitated by the rapid advance of civilisation, and by the introduction of improved and modern systems of Government, promises to entail a large progressive expenditure which cannot be overtaken except with the assistance of increasing revenue from the land. This argument does not appear to be sound. The existing complex machinery of administration, however efficient in theory and practice, is unsuited to the poor people of India for several reasons, the chief of which is its costliness. It therefore stands to reason that the cost of that administration should not be further enhanced at the expense of the poor. There are other sources of revenue besides the land—for instance, stamps, excise, assessed taxes, registration, etc.,—which contribute materially to the ever-growing needs of the Government. It is those heads of revenue, rather than the land, that are indicative of material prosperity; and the additional annual charge for the administration ought to be defrayed out of those expansive heads. The poor and the famine-stricken, who rely mainly on the soil, should not be laid under a heavy contribution for administrative reforms unless they are directly calculated to their advantage. It may be easily admitted that land is the most extensive and most prolific source of public revenue; but, at the same time, it must not be forgotten that calls on the land for the exigencies of administration have not only been more frequent and persistent, but have been more readily responded to than calls on trades, professions and industries. The simple reason is that it is less difficult to raise revenue from the land than from any other source. This is one of the considerations which should rather deter than induce the Government to raise further taxation by revisions of settlements. As felicitously expressed by Sir Louis Mallet "the Settlement Department may be designated the great Unsettlement Department of the Government"; and unless its revisional operations are stopped, peace and prosperity will not be secured to the people and to the country. Every desire to meet the increasing cost of administration from progressive land revenue should be finally given up, and the Government should evince a practical solicitude for the peasantry by conferring on them a boon by which peace, wealth and happiness will be assured to them. His Majesty's Government has decided to reduce the cultivation of the poppy in India by one-tenth every year and ultimately to forego the whole of the opium revenue of 6 crores of rupees as a concession to the clamour of the temperance reformers in Great Britain. This decision is singularly inconsistent with the persistence with which the same Government maintain the existing excise system and defend the revision settlements in this country.

Refutation of the argument that Permanent Settlement is no remedy.

It has been alleged that the Permanent Settlement is no remedy for the prevention of famines and it is argued that Bengal, the land of the Permanent Settlement, has not been immune from such calamities within the last 100 years. In the celebrated resolution of the 16th January, 1902, which the Hon'ble Sir Edward Baker calls "the *locus classicus* of the Government of India in respect of land revenue administration," an endeavour is made to belittle the importance of that great measure by stating that "neither these advantages nor the Permanent Settlement have availed to save Bengal from serious drought when the monsoon failure. from which it is ordinarily free, has spread to that part of India. Omitting to notice the frequent earlier famines, that known as the Bihar famine of 1873-74 . . . cost the State £6,000,000; while it can be shown that in the famine of 1897, there were, at the height of distress, considerably more than $\frac{3}{4}$ million persons on relief in the permanently settled districts of Bengal, and that the total cost of that famine to the Bengal administration was Rs. 1,08,04,000 or £720,266, as compared with a famine expenditure of Rs. 98,28,000 or £655,200 in Madras, and Rs. 1,26,37,000 or £843,466 in Bombay; and this, although the daily cost of each person was less." These figures will strike the reader who is familiar with official statistics and the circumstances connected with the Bihar famine of 1873-74, as most delusive. In the first place, it will be remembered in what reckless and injudicious a scale famine relief was administered in Bihar in 1873. Owing to the lack of statistical information regarding the number and requirements of the distressed population the estimates were both fallacious and uncertain. This ignorance led in Orissa "to the refusal of relief to a starving population," and it led in 1874 "to the lavishing of relief on a population, which (to a large extent, at least) was not only not starving, but which was hardly even distressed." Relief tests were either relaxed or altogether neglected; purchases of grain, much in excess of requirements, were made at State expense and on State responsibility; and the waste and extravagance that resulted account for a substantial portion of the recorded expenditure of six millions. Sir John Strachey, an unquestioned authority on famine finance, stated that, owing to the profound ignorance in Bengal of agricultural affairs, the effect on the finances and the administrative system of Government was most serious; and in Saran, "the original estimate on which the relief measures of the Government were based, was in excess of the actual loss by 100 per cent. A similar error occurred in regard to the district of Gya where the area under winter rice was estimated at 75 per cent. of the whole cultivated area, whereas, in reality, it was hardly more than 50 per cent." "The result of these accumulated errors," he continued, "was the mistaken belief that a terrible famine must be impending, and more than £700,000 (seventy lakhs of rupees) was expended, for the most part, needlessly on famine relief in Saran alone......I state within careful limits, when I state my deliberate conviction, that a knowledge of the cultivated area of crops and of average yield in Bengal ......would have saved the State millions of pounds sterling in 1874." It is herein admitted on the highest official authority of the day, that the cost of the Bihar famine of 1873, represented by six millions, is not only exaggerated by "millions" (as stated by Sir John) but is highly fictitious. An administration of that famine under the present system and tests, and with a previous correct knowledge of facts would, therefore, have reduced the cost to a fraction of what it actually was. The situation is eloquently described in an extract from an esteemed Anglo-Indian paper which is quoted in Appendix C.

In the second place, the aggravating cause of the famine in Bihar was the depressed and impoverished condition of the tenantry brought about by rack-renting, oppression and the illegal action of the landlords. From the extract given in Appendix C from Sir C. P. Ilbert's speech introducing the Bengal Tenancy Bill in the Governor-General's Council, it will be seen that the landlords in Bihar, unlike those in Eastern Bengal, were strong and the tenants weak. The Permanent Settlement of 1793 did not provide any ready means of enabling the tenantry to protect themselves from the illegal restraint, illegal enhancement of rent, and illegal cesses, and to prove and maintain their customary and occupancy rights, of which they were in enjoyment at the time of the Permanent Settlement. These evils were not adequately provided for by the measure of 1793, and they effectually arrested the development of agricultural prosperity, and practically placed the tenants at the mercy of the landlords. It is this condition of agrarian poverty and agricultural depression, caused by the high-handedness and lawless actions of the landlords, that aggravated the physical effects of the drought of 1873 in Bihar. If the pledge held out at the Settlement of 1793, to which fuller reference will be made later on, had been redeemed, the economic condition of the Bihar tenantry would have been far more prosperous in 1873-4 than was actually the case, and the disastrous consequences of the famine would, in a great measure, have been counteracted by the greater resisting capacity of the people. It is obvious, from the above *resumé* of circumstances, that if we eliminated the two potent factors which magnified the proportions of the Bihar famine, *viz.*, the omissions of the Permanent Settlement and the blunders in the administration of famine relief, we should probably find that the Bihar famine, of which such an appalling account has been given in official reports, would be reduced to nothing more than a local scarcity.

The second part of the extract from the Resolution of the 16th January quoted above suggests that the famine in Bengal which occurred in 1897 was as intense and widespread as either the Madras or Bombay famine of the same year, or at least, that Bengal was as equally liable to famine as its two sister provinces. I have compiled, in Appendix B, certain statistics which mathematically demonstrate that the percentage of total units relieved, and of the average daily number of people on relief, to the population of the distressed area, was the lowest in Bengal ; and the percentage of the maximum number on relief to the latter was the lowest in that province, with the exception of Bombay. It will also be seen that with the exception of the United Provinces, where labour is exceedingly cheap, the cost of relief per 1,000 units relieved was the lowest in Bengal, the cost in Bombay and Madras being 30 per cent. higher. From these results we are justified in concluding that the resisting power of the people of Bengal is higher than in any other province; and that, under given conditions, the people of Bengal are less in need of relief than the people of any other province. The value of the benefits conferred by the Permanent Settlement is not altogether a negligible quantity, and there is no reason to doubt that a similar measure applied to the rest of India, under proper safeguards, will be attended with greater beneficial results than it has been in Bengal.

It has been further asserted in the Resolution that the Permanent Settlement has not, as it is claimed for it, converted the position of the Bengal tenants " into one of exceptional comfort and prosperity." It is argued that " precisely because this was *not* the case, and because so far from being generously treated by the zemindars, the Bengal cultivators were rack-rented, impoverished and oppressed, that the Government of India felt compelled to intervene on their behalf, and, by the series of legislative measures that commenced with the Bengal Act of 1859, and culminated in the Act of 1885, to place them in the position of greater security which they now enjoy. To confound this legislation with the Permanent Settlement, and ascribe, even in part, to the latter the benefits which it had conspicuously failed to confer, and which would never have accrued but for the former, is strangely to misread history." No attempt will be made here to trace the development of the agrarian situation in Bengal from 1793 to 1859 when the first Act, giving greater security to the Bengal tenants, was passed. It is well known why the necessity for further legislation in the same direction was recognised. The most superficial reader of agrarian history of Bengal which preceded the enactment of the legislation of 1885 is familiar with the fact that successive Indian administrators either failed or neglected to redeem a pledge, which had been given about three-quarters of a century ago, " to protect," in the words of the Regulation of 1793, " all classes of people and more particularly those who, from their situation, are most helpless "; and to enact such regulations as the Governor-General in Council might think necessary " for the protection and welfare of the dependent taluqdars, ryots and other cultivators of the soil." The Acts of 1859 and 1885 merely embody this pledge and define the mutual rights of the zemindars and ryots which the Regulation of 1793 did not define. These Acts were enacted with the object of correcting the errors, supplying the omissions of the Permanent Settlement, and settling the outstanding rights left undefined in 1793. They are, in fact, supplementary to, and a commentary on, the Regulation I of 1793. Instead, therefore, of asserting that they should not be confounded with the Permanent Settlement, it would be appropriate to say that these three legislative measures, passed in three different periods, constitute, together, the Great Permanent Settlement of Bengal and a Charter of the rights of those who have either a direct or indirect interest in the soil. The point of argument is not whether the Permanent Settlement of Lord Cornwallis has failed to confer benefits on the people; but whether, in spite of its errors and omissions, the condition of the peasantry in Bengal is not comparatively more prosperous than in the rest of India; and, whether, if a Settlement was now introduced under proper safeguards, it would not be materially better than that in Bengal. The Permanent Settlement, which is now suggested to be introduced, is not the Settlement tainted with the defects of the first great experiment, but one which is free from the mistakes of the past, perfect in its practical working, recognising the rights and interests of the subordinate landholders, and framed in the light of our latest knowledge under the guidance of experienced, judicious, and sympathetic advisers. Such a Settlement will, it is hoped, secure to the ryot all the advantages that are claimed for it, and it is in such a Settlement that he hopes to find his salvation. The Government of India, in their resolution of the 16th January 1902, do not, of course, admit that the Permanent Settlement is a protection either against the incidence or the consequences of famine; but there is manifest, in the whole tenor of the resolution, a latent recognition of the proposition that moderation in assessments and long-term Settlements are conducive to the well-being of the cultivators. A logical extension of this proposition is that the Permanent Settlement, under certain safeguards, will permanently improve the condition of the people and will give them greater capacity for resistance against the effects of famine.

I trust I shall not be accused of an unwarrantable digression in criticising a resolution of the Supreme Government in the course of an essay on famine. But I feel I am justified in defending my theory that the Permanent Settlement is, at least, one of the measures which confers a certain amount of resourcefulness and resisting power on the people to enable them to withstand the disastrous effects of a physical calamity. And, if in defending that theory I have endeavoured to prove that the contrary theory is unsound, the attitude will not, perhaps, be regarded as one of hostility.

Extension of Railways and Irrigation a remedy.

The other protective measures which have, at various times, been suggested for the prevention or mitigation of famine are the extension of railways and irrigation. Activity of traffic and perfection of communication established by railways have promptly responded to the emergency arising during famine by the maintenance of a uniform level of prices throughout the country, and by allowing the trade to adjust the supply to the demand. The extension of railways in India has been carried out at a rate much in excess of that recommended by the Famine Commissioners of 1880. In that year the total length of open lines was 9,000 miles. The maximum length which the Commissioners considered would give security to the country was 20,000 miles. At the beginning of the current year the mileage of open lines was 32,744 miles. The recommendations of the Famine Commission have therefore been more than sufficiently carried out, and the railways may be said to have amply fulfilled their mission in the campaigns of the Government against famine. Both the Famine Commissions of 1898 and 1901 recommended that a more prominent place should be given to irrigation than to railways in any future programme of famine insurance. A Commission was accordingly appointed by a resolution of the Government of India dated the 13th September 1901, to ascertain, among other matters, the scope which exists for the further extension of irrigation works, the desirability of stimulating private enterprise in the construction of private land-improvement works with State assistance, and the utility of irrigation under local conditions of agriculture, whether in generally increasing the produce of the land or in securing from the effects of failure of rainfall. In considering proposals for new irrigation works, the Commission was asked to consider whether they would be likely to prove financially profitable, and whether the net burden which they might impose on the State in the form of charges for interest and maintenance would be too high a price to pay for the protection against famine which they might be relied on to afford. These points have been exhaustively dealt with, with special reference to drought and its consequences, by the Commission. They recommend a wide, but not an unlimited, extension of irrigation works in every province, at a total cost of 44 crores of rupees, to be spread over a number of years; and with reference to the question of profitable investments *versus* protective values they estimate that the burden on the State will be relieved—

(1) by the reduction in the future cost of famine which will result from this expenditure;
(2) by the cultivation on these works which will reduce the cost of famine in other ways;
(3) by contributing to the share in the increase of the wealth of the community which will accrue to the State indirectly in all years.

As regards extension of State irrigation works it must, of course, be admitted that the number of remunerative works is limited and will eventually be exhausted; but they do not propose any final limit to the expenditure which may be legitimately incurred by the Government in preventing distress. They recognise that in this object is involved the well-being of millions who, in all but the most unfavourable years, add to the revenues of the State and to the wealth of the country by precarious cultivation which they carry on in unprotected tracts.

The subject of granting loans and advances to agriculturists in order to enable them to execute private irrigational improvements, such as the construction of wells, water-courses, etc., is dealt with by the Commission in a liberal and sympathetic spirit. They recommend, on the basis of the opinions of experienced and well-qualified officers of the Government, that a free grant of 17 lakhs, and a grant for *taqavi* loans of 58 lakhs (total 75 lakhs), should be annually provided in the "Ways and Means Estimate" of the Government of India, subject to the revision of the grant every five years, and suggest that a universal rate of 5 per cent. should be charged on the principle that the State should not look for direct financial profit on such transactions. It is believed that this rate will cover all risks contingent on the irrecoverability of the loans. Reference is also made to the unpopularity of the *taqavi* advances due to the endless delay and trouble which seem to be inseparable from official procedure and to the exactions of underlings. To enhance the popularity of the loans, they recommend that an officer of standing should advance money on the spot, and the journeys of applicants to headquarters should either be shortened or saved. The Commissioners conclude with the following observations: "It is more important to realise what irrigation can do than what it cannot. The whole of India can never be protected from famine by irrigation alone, but irrigation can do much to restrict the area and to mitigate the intensity of famines. We cannot but repeat, in respect of the measures that we propose, the wise warnings of the last Famine Commission that their enduring success will depend no less on their effect in evolving a spirit of self-help and thrift among the people than on their efficiency in securing the crops from drought. Nevertheless, we hope that if they are vigorously and systematically carried to completion, they will at least give all the protection from drought that irrigation is capable of affording; and that the additional security thereby conferred on the agricultural classes of India may tend to develop amongst them that prudence and practice of thrift without which irrigation of itself will be of little permanent or lasting value."

It is superfluous to suggest further or better remedies connected with irrigation beyond those recommended by the Irrigation Commission. Their recommendations leave nothing to be desired, either in point of comprehensiveness of programme or breadth of view, either in thoroughness of detail or liberality of spirit. It is a matter of regret, however, that the Government has not yet been able to give full effect to these recommendations; and, while the railway grant has been considerably swelled of late by contribution from the Gold Reserve Fund, not only has not the grant recommended for irrigation been fully provided, but the annual provision has not been actually spent for some years past. If, however, the recommendations are not overlooked and are faithfully given effect to, a great advance will have been made in extending cultivation, in augmenting agricultural wealth, and in securing protection from drought; and the Report will stand as a landmark in the history of famine prevention in India.

Disforestation—a cause of famine.

During the thirty years that followed the famine of 1876-77, great strides have been made in the extension of the area under cultivation. The process cannot be viewed as one of unmixed good to the country. On the one hand, it has brought extensive areas under the plough and added considerably to the agricultural wealth of the country; on the other, it has denuded vast tracts of country of a valuable stock of national wealth, which it will take years to replenish. The value and advantages of the one cannot be precisely weighed against the evils and disadvantages of the other; but one fact stands out prominent in the situation, namely, that, when disforestation is carried out on a large scale whole tracts of the country are exposed to the heat of the tropical sun, and the absorbent property of the cleanings as well as of the surrounding lands is immensely reduced. The storage of moisture in the soil of the country as a whole diminishes, and the best conditions of agriculture for the rest of the country, which would have benefited cultivation by seepage and transpiration, are not realised. Extension of agriculture and denudation of forests thus act and react upon each other, and the interests of one department are sometimes looked upon as encroaching on the interests of the other. It will, it is apprehended, be discovered some day that in an agricultural country like ours, commerce and industry are being unduly fostered at the expense, and to the detriment, of agriculture. Though amid the headlong progress of civilisation, these actions cannot be effectively controlled, yet, it will strike the observer that the effect of the clearance of forests on the soil and the climate is most pernicious. As national assets, forests are of great value; and they should be economised to the best advantage of the country. Their value, relative to their influence on agriculture, is enhanced by the fact that their wanton destruction results in a deterioration of the nutrient properties of the soil by making evaporation more rapid and depriving it of its slow and continual nourishment which is supplied through streams and rivers—the natural agencies of irrigation. They also exert an enormous influence on the physical characteristics of the country. In India specially, where physical circumstances profoundly affect its rural economy, their importance cannot be too highly overrated. In Lower Bengal the effect of the denudation is not likely, at least for some considerable time to come, to be very serious; because the country is too moist by reason of its low level, of its proximity to the sea, and of the innumerable water-courses that intersect it, to need entire dependence on rainfall. In the high lands, however, where the humidity of the atmosphere and moisture in the soil are essential factors of successful cultivation during a period of drought, the matter deserves most careful attention and systematic investigation. The question whether forests have any influence on the quantity and regularity of rainfall is, to a certain extent, controversial; and, it is impossible to assert, with scientific precision, that rainfall depends upon forests. But the experience and opinion of many experts (quoted in Appendix D) who have carefully observed natural phenomena, point to the inference that precipitation does, to a great extent, vary with the existence and density of forests, that in a region where rainfall was abundant when it was covered with forests, it has markedly diminished after it has been shorn of its timber, and conversely that re-afforestation of a barren country has increased its rainfall. As an illustration, I quote the following from an esteemed newspaper: "It appears that the Russian

Government planted a large number of trees—chiefly elms and poplars—in a certain district in Central Asia. The result was that rainfall exceeded by 250 per cent. Referring to this fact, Lieutenant-General Forrest, writing to a Bombay contemporary, protests against the consumption of wood as fuel in the 43 mills at Ahmedabad, where the rainfall has been extremely deficient during the past two years." In a recent article in the *Indian Forester*, the writer says that balloonists have noticed a remarkable diminution of temperature while passing over extensive forest areas as high up as 4,000 or 5,000 feet. It is therefore obvious that "if forests cause a decrease in temperature to such a considerable height, rain-bearing clouds passing over the land would, on meeting the cooler belt of air above the forest, probably often be induced to precipitate rain....... The cool air given off by the forests would be carried on by whatever air current were moving at the time, and this cool air would tend to decrease the general temperature of the air even above the surrounding parts of the country where no forests existed; and the general tendency would be to render the condition of the atmosphere more favourable for inducing precipitation should rain-bearing clouds pass over." The statistics of rainfall in India confirm this view, for they show that it is heaviest in the cool and forest-clad mountainous regions of the north in which the principal rivers,—which distribute the fertilising fluid throughout Northern India—take their rise. The northern regions of India are most liable to deficiency of rainfall, most dependent on irrigation and most vulnerable to famine. It is unfortunately in the mountainous regions of India—the source of our great rivers—that the extermination of forests is proceeding at a ruthless and accelerating rate. What the effects of this wanton extermination will be, no one can pretend to foresee; but if we are to judge from observed phenomena we may conclude that they are destined to be very disastrous.

The influence of forests on the rainfall of India, and therefore indirectly on agriculture, is of supreme importance from the point of view of the famine administrator. The arrangements provided by nature appear to be based on principles of perfect economy, and human beings ought to act prudently by making the most of these arrangements without violently and unnecessarily disturbing the balance of Nature. A national forest is a capital of slow growth; and, if once destroyed, it cannot be replaced in a generation or two. The Forest Department of the Government of India was established more than 40 years ago with the special object of conserving the forests which, in certain parts of India, were then in course of ruthless and complete destruction. In the early fifties no systematic effort was made for the conservation of forests, and the Government did not anticipate that the spread of the civilising agencies would make the destruction so thoughtless and rapid. "We officers of the Government believed," complained Mr. Pedder of the India Office, "that as there had always been forests in India, so there always would be; that they did not require any particular conservation, but that natural reproduction was quite sufficient for them, and that they would grow again by themselves. We did not at the time appreciate the enormous destruction caused to the Indian forests by the spread of cultivation which has almost doubled itself in many parts of India, besides the demand of the railways for wood, and the great demand arising in large cities, such as Bombay and Calcutta on their being brought into easy communication with forests by railways and harbours, in which there is an immense demand for timber, specially for firewood." In spite of this complaint, which was made about 40 years ago, the loss of forests during this period has been enormous. The policy hitherto pursued by the Government of India in regard to forest conservation has not been inspired by sympathy for the greatest industry of India—but for the subsidiary industries. In what satisfactory manner the Government can adjust the conflicting claims of agriculture and commerce, it is not for me to advise. But there is no question that the matter deserves serious consideration. I can only suggest that the effects of the violent hand of man on the forests should be carefully and scientifically observed and investigated by the Meteorological Department, which has as yet done little useful or substantial work, and measures should be taken to prevent them. The task devolving upon the Meteorological Department in the suggested sphere of activity would be more real, more practical, and fraught with greater benefits to the country, than that on which it has hitherto spent its funds and energies. The department is akin to an experimental class for the observation of natural phenomena and for the deduction of results therefrom. This should be the function of an education rather than an administrative department. I beg to suggest that the experimental branch of the department be separated from the administrative branch, and that a forest expert be added to it to evolve a scheme by which some practical work in the direction indicated can be accomplished, which will enhance the natural beauty and the national capital of India.

Emigration.

The next important remedy that has been generally proposed is emigration. But in a country where about 200 millions of people are affected, it must be resorted to on a gigantic scale in order that the remedy must be effective. The idea of emigration is an evolution of Western civilisation under the influence of which primitive and undeveloped continents were sought after in different parts of the world for the dumping of the surplus and unemployed population of the mother country. This idea of colonial emigration on a large scale is wholly alien to the Indian mind and is, moreover, politically impracticable. Where is the country, for instance, which can be settled by a million or two of Indian peasants where they can live according to their own style of comfort and civilisation without undue interference with their customs and habits? It is not always that Western systems fructify in Eastern lands, neither is it always good statesmanship to apply to India economic theories which are not appreciated by, and are unknown to, the people of this country, because experience has found them to be workable and beneficial in European countries. Foreign emigration must therefore be left out of account as distasteful to the people, and liable to be resented on social grounds. As to inland emigration, the only successful scheme within recent times is the colonisation scheme in the Punjab. It has brought extensive areas under the plough and has increased the productive capacity and the agricultural wealth of the country by millions of rupees. But it is a political scheme, and the number of settlers is far too small to materially affect the condition of the labouring classes as a whole.

In para. 9 of the Resolution in the Revenue and Agriculture Department of the 19th October 1888, the Government of India anticipated enormous possibilities from the recent addition to the Empire of a large tract of new country. They did not doubt that "the annexation of Upper Burma will help to solve the problem of relieving congested tracts of India on a scale and in a manner which could never have been obtained by emigration to the limited and unhealthy area of the Central Provinces"; and they thought it expedient that "attention should be chiefly directed to that country as the possible field for relieving over-population in India." It is needless to say that neither the Government nor the affected population of India displayed any enthusiasm in the matter, and the anticipations have never been, nor will ever be, realised. The greatest obstacle to a successful scheme of emigration in India is, in the words of the Famine Commission of 1880, the absence of the "peculiar energy and spirit of enterprise which are requisite to stimulate emigration to a distant country in the hope of a higher standard of material comfort." They recommended, however, in spite of its unpopularity and the difficulties surrounding it, that the Government should endeavour to frame and carry out "a scheme of emigration designed with a scientific care to meet the physical wants and the mental and moral idiosyncrasies of the Indian agricultural population." But as it is well known that the Indian peasant is perversely reluctant to abandon his cherished field and to settle down in a foreign or distant country, the idea of a scheme of wholesale emigration is unattainable in practice. Moreover, as stated before, nothing short of a scheme of colossal proportions, organised and carried out at enormous cost, which the Government will unhesitatingly refuse to take on its shoulders, will provide field for more than a very small fraction of the population and afford sensible relief to over-population in congested districts. Education of the people and better times for the Government are necessary to carry out a practical scheme of the kind suggested. The time seems to be yet far distant when emigration can be suggested as a successful remedy for the prevention of famine caused by the pressure of population on the land.

Agricultural Statistics.

In dwelling on the effects of the Permanent Settlement on the condition of the peasantry, reference was made to the absence of reliable agricultural statistics in Bengal. This defect may be predicated generally of the remaining provinces. These statistics, where they exist, are so incomplete and unreliable as to be useless for the purpose of determining the economy of rural life. Calculations have, at various times, been made on what are untrustworthy and conjectural data, to find out whether the income of the mass of the population is increasing or diminishing, and whether that income is generally adequate, in the circumstances of the country, for the sustenance of life. The opposing schools of economists who are responsible for these two theories are unable to confidently assert that his theory is correct because of the hypothetical character of the data; and the result is that either party condemns the conclusion of the other as erroneous. This leads to loss of confidence in the accuracy of the calculations and to irritating contentions. Detailed agricultural statistics, in which must be included population, area under crops, their outturn, value, wastage, consumption and requirements, advances by Government, agricultural indebtedness, domestic economy, extent of the ryot's dependence on the money-lender, etc., are not only of value on account of their usefulness as a guide to trade, but also for purposes of famine relief and general administration. In the words of Sir Charles Elliott they would afford a "basis for conclusions as to the reasonableness of the assessment of land-revenue, and the fiscal history of each village would be a record at the time of resettlement."

Statistics carefully compiled for the supply of detailed and accurate information on the above points do not at present exist anywhere in the published papers. It is hoped that the new Department of Agriculture will not only arrange to collect and collate such statistics in a complete and useful form, but will also publish them for general information. It must not, of course, be understood that statistical information of the nature indicated above will operate directly as a preventive of famine; but its indirect value in acquainting the Government and the public with an idea of the resources and needs of the people and of the country as a whole, will be of the greatest help to enable the Government to determine the nature of the remedy required and to estimate, with a great deal of accuracy, the staying power of the former in times of scarcity, and to adopt prompt preventive measures whenever the necessity for them arises. There is efficient machinery at the disposal of the Government for the preparation of such statistics; and unless there are some weaknesses to hide, there is ample justification for their preparation, especially when opinions so widely vary regarding the economic condition of the peasantry. In a matter of such vital importance, the public and the Government should not be left to speculate, when all doubts on the subject can be set at rest by setting the Government machinery in motion.

Promotion of agriculture.

Intimately associated with the question of the improvement of agricultural statistics are the subjects of the propagation of agricultural instruction, the development of agriculture and agricultural industries, and the diversification of industrial occupations. The two subjects—agriculture and industries—may, in the economic development of India, be considered together, inasmuch as agriculture has been called the greatest of Indian industries. Within the last 5 or 6 years, the Government of India have done much to develop agriculture in this country; but I will venture to say that much yet remains to be done both as regards the lines along which their policy should be directed and as regards the amount of funds required for its full development. During the above period the Imperial Government increased the grant for agricultural development and research from the modest figure of a lakh and a half to the handsome figure of 25 lakhs of rupees; and the public have been assured that this increased grant is "another step in furtherance of the policy on which we have embarked of rendering *whatever assistance it may be in the power of the State to afford to the principal industry of the country*." But this qualified assurance is not enough. It is, as I will show later on, in the power of the Government, under present circumstances, to afford all necessary aid for the promotion of agriculture in the same liberal scale on which funds have been provided for such services as the army, the police, and the railways. The only difference in the attitude of Government is the difference in the spirit of expenditure dominant in each case. Expenditure on agriculture is a far more profitable investment than expenditure on railways or other public works, for with cheap labour and vast expanses of land, it requires a comparatively smaller outlay to reproduce national wealth than industry.

The public have persistently complained that in spite of the stimulus imparted six years ago, agricultural development has been very slow in this country. The Hon. Sir D. Ibbetson explained that this must necessarily be the case as there was no want of money but of men. He said that both in the matter of trained agency and in the matter of teaching staff we must begin at the top and work downwards. "Our first necessity," he continued, "is a number of highly-trained English-speaking Indians who will prepare the necessary text-books, in the vernacular, and who, in turn, will instruct vernacular-speaking teachers to be employed in the lower grades of training institutions and schools. In the Budget debate of last year, I said that I hoped that the Pusa scheme, which has been fully described in a recently published resolution, would prove to be the corner-stone of agricultural progress in India." Arrangements have, I understand, been completed to start the Pusa Institute; but one feels inclined to complain that Sir D. Ibbetson's proposals lack much practical value in a country where knowledge has to be imparted to the agriculturists in their vernacular. Agricultural instruction cannot claim its proper value if it degenerates into theoretical education or into a mere medium for the diffusion of text-books. It must reach the masses by means of practical object-lessons carried on by a sufficient number of village headmen or zemindars. The development must begin simultaneously at the bottom as well as at the top. The object of the Pusa Institute is declared to be that the "expert staff shall conduct higher lines of research applicable to all India and beyond the capacity of the Provincial Departments, guide and assist the provincial experts in their several branches, train young scientists for future employment as provincial experts, and be the professors of the higher grade agricultural colleges for India." The scheme outlined above would be sound and practical if the Government had a small and compact community to deal with. Agricultural education in every country has been attended with marked success wherever the superior agencies have been in close touch with the people whom it is designed to educate in the fundamental principles of the art and science of agriculture. The organisation described above is eminently unsuited to the present urgent needs of India. It seems to me that, considering the large army of teachers required to impart instruction in agricultural schools throughout the country, and the millions of people to be instructed, the scheme will take half a century to mature, and the real solid and useful work of reform must begin 50 years hence. Besides, the organisation, I apprehend, is defective in one essential point. The results of the work, conducted as it will be by an expert staff of Europeans, will be of a highly scientific and theoretical character and will be communicated by means of a subordinate staff to the agriculturists in a form incapable of understanding and unsuitable for practice. Practical instruction in the methods of agricultural improvement requires constant personal intercourse between the instructive staff and the villagers. The teaching imparted should also be clear, intelligible to the meanest capacity, and free from all pedantic technicalities. But the scheme outlined above is too ambitious and technical to aim at these essential requirements of agricultural instruction, and the time, money and labour that will be spent in manufacturing a huge army of instructors and in establishing hundreds of schools will be of no immediate benefit to the people.

There are at present two schools (Cawnpore and Nagpur) and three colleges (Madras, Sibpur and Poona) which impart higher agricultural instruction. "The function of the schools is to train the higher class of land revenue officials. At the colleges, the instruction is more theoretical than practical, and the course leads to a diploma or a degree." As a rule, these educational institutions afford passports to Government or other employment, and profess no sympathy with the wants of the agriculturists as a class. In addition to these schools and colleges there are experimental farms at some 12 towns in the different provinces where agricultural experiments are conducted by third-rate investigators on a very humble scale with more or less success. Beyond publishing the results of their investigations, they evince no practical solicitude for educating the people of the neighbourhood. Those that are fortunate enough to glean a meagre knowledge of the value of certain manures, or the culture of certain plants and vegetables under certain conditions of soil and climate, generally fail in their independent efforts to follow the vague and unpractical instructions contained in the reports, and gradually lose confidence in their value. The interested millions that do not see these reports are never taught their contents. Owing to the theoretical and exclusive character of the operations conducted by these agricultural institutions, they have hitherto exerted very little educative influence on the progress of agriculture in this country. One,therefore, grows sceptic about the future success of the Pusa Institute whose influence on the general diffusion of agricultural knowledge in the country will be only remote and indirect. A more practical and effective scheme would be to begin at the bottom and develop upwards: namely, to provide for a course of elementary agricultural instruction in primary schools. Elementary text-books, containing simple and general lessons, can be prepared by the existing staff without difficulty; and when the village boys have imbibed a taste for improved agricultural methods, the way to higher and more scientific training will be made clearer and easier. A move has recently been made in the Central Provinces which promises to simplify and popularise the methods of agricultural instruction in that province. It combines, in brief, primary instruction of the masses with a practical course of lessons in agriculture by means of object-lessons, and inaugurates a judicious departure for the popularisation and dissemination of elementary practical instruction in agricultural science. In Holland, horticulture and market-gardening are taught in certain winter schools where general instruction is given so as to suit the conditions of each province. In France, agricultural associations in Brittany have started a movement for imparting elementary agricultural instruction in the primary schools, and they award certificates and diplomas to the successful children. In Poland, gardens are attached to primary schools where children may learn the rudiments of gardening and the care of fruit trees which are planted by themselves. In the United States "the introduction of agricultural subjects into the schedules of nature study, now so widely adopted in the elementary schools throughout the country, is progressing rapidly, and there is much interest in the establishment of school gardens in connection with such study. The idea of diffusing a general elementary knowledge of agriculture and gardening through primary schools appears to me to be a method which is not only eminently practical in its operation, but is admirably suited to the needs and conditions of India. It has been introduced into the Central Provinces after the experience of two severe famines, and it may be introduced into the rest of India with immediate beneficial results to the agricultural community.

A distinguished official of the Canadian Government once said: "No business or calling in life offers better opportunities for intelligent and well-directed efforts than agriculture"; and "with this industry in a healthy condition, all other industries will soon feel the benefit." In no country in the world do these observations apply with greater pertinence than in India. The welfare of the country and the very existence of the people, are so inseparably bound up with agriculture that it should have the foremost claims on the public revenues. The vital importance of agriculture to the people and the State was never more admirably or emphatically stated than by Sir D. M. Hamilton. "The ryot," he said, "pays the land-revenue, and the bulk of the salt tax; the ryot's labour yields the opium revenue. The ryot pays the best part of the excise income, and all the other branches of revenue are, more or less, dependent on his labours. The ryot fills the railway wagons, and fills the steamers; the ryot grows the jute and fills the gunny bags; the ryot grows the cotton and wears the manufactured cloth. In short, to quote the ancient sage 'the profit of the earth is for all: the King himself is served by the field.'" Agricultural prospects in this country have impressed the imagination of a British merchant; but a Government which has allowed the agriculture of its own nation to deteriorate and decay, out of a blind faith in the Free Trade gospel, looks on the prospects of a purely agricultural country through a dazzling blaze of industrial and commercial prosperity. Up to this time the Government of India have dealt with the problem in a sympathetic, though not in a thoroughly liberal, spirit; and the funds provided have been miserably inadequate to supply the needs of a population of 190 millions spread over an area of one million square miles. It would therefore be interesting to contrast the nature and amount of State aid to agriculture in India with that in certain foreign countries.

The Canadian Government sends periodically experts to Great Britain and Ireland to ascertain how to extend the markets for Canadian products; and when they return home they publish the results of their investigation. Experts employed by the Government give advice as to the rotation of crops, analysis of soil, destruction of weeds and pests, breeding, preparation of dairy products, curing of meat, orchard cultivation, and various other useful matters connected with agriculture. These advices are given free, and letters addressed to the Agricultural Department pass through the mails in the Dominion free of charge. The State makes a grant-in-aid of £:00 to every society in Ontario established for the purpose of importing "valuable live-stock, grain, seed, useful implements, or whatever else might conduce to the improvement of agriculture," provided the society itself raised one-quarter of the grant. There are also farmers' institutes, which are being rapidly spread throughout the Dominion. Each local institute receives a grant of 25 dollars under the legislature on condition that an equal sum is granted by the County Council or the District Municipal Board. The object of the local institutes is to disseminate agricultural knowledge in the district and to develop local talent. The officers " endeavour to bring the rank and file of farmers into touch with the most successful local men, that the masses may become more conversant with the best and most profitable methods." The results of these concessions have proved highly beneficial to the community, and their educative value has been incalculable.

In the United States, the operations of the Agricultural Department, which are more extensive, co-operative and practical, are disseminated through the Experimental Stations, which now number about 60, and through farmers' institutes. Of these 60 institutes 53 receive State grants aggregating one million dollars. As an illustration of the increase of production accomplished with the help of these experimental stations, it may be pointed out that a new variety of oats has been introduced, and the result has been a general increase of yield of from 3 to 5 bushels per acre. In the Wisconsin district alone, this new variety has yielded a gain to the farmers of from 2½ million to 4½ million dollars a year. Again, "the reports of experiments with Tappahannock wheat, distributed by the department, show an average yield of 25 bushels. The total yield, at that rate, on the acreage of 1898, would be 461,503,300 bushels, an increase of 237,466,700 bushels, which at 1·42 dollars per bushel would be a money-value increase of 337,202,714 dollars. If this wheat were to take the place of other varieties, however, and should be sown as the general crop is now sown, without the special care in experimenting, the average yield would, of course, fall below 25 bushels; but if the average increase per acre could be raised to 15 bushels (a low estimate for the Tappahannock) the increase in bushels would be 55,380,396, in money-value, 78,640,162 dollars." Another evidence of the useful work done by the farms is afforded by the application of insecticides and fungicides as means of cereal and fruit protection. In the Wisconsin station 25,000 farmers resorted to a method of treatment of oat smuts, and it is estimated that the loss averted in this district alone has amounted to between 3 to 7 million dollars a year. "When the Hatch Act was passed, it was estimated that the annual value of agricultural produce in the United States was 3 billions of dollars. The census of 1900 shows that the annual output of farmers now amount to 5 billions of dollars. It is believed that the experimental stations have had much to do with our increased agricultural production. The funds expended in their maintenance have thus proved to be highly remunerative investments."

It is impossible to enumerate in brief the different lines along which the investigations of the farms are conducted; but it may be stated generally that no branch of economics in which land plays a part is neglected, and no money or trouble is spared to ensure what is called "economic self-sufficiency" by growing tropical fruits, plants and fibres, etc., for which the States depend on foreign countries to the extent of 200 million dollars a year. Explorations, for instance, have been made into Algeria with the object of introducing an alfalfa adapted to certain arid tracts in the south-west. The seed secured has been planted, and it is expected that with this plant it will be possible to reclaim vast areas of alkaline lands in the country. The wide range and variety of matters investigated shows that no subject is considered too insignificant to receive careful and systematic scientific attention.

In Victoria, New South Wales, Queensland, South and West Australia, and in New Zealand, legislative and executive measures have been adopted to finance agriculturists. The active support given by the State has placed the necessary funds within their easy reach, and has thus advanced the industry by leaps and bounds within the last few years.

In Hungary 3,700,000 acres of State forests, 3,000,000 acres of communal forests, and about 9 million acres belonging to private corporations are managed by the Minister of Agriculture. "To encourage the replanting of forests and barren territories, the State distributed between 1883 and 1901 no fewer than 358 millions of shoots free of charge. The revival of viticulture in Hungary after the phyllexora devastations in the seventies, was mainly due to the action of the State which encouraged the transformation of 100,000 acres of barren sandy waste into vineyards with American grapes, and established 2,500 acres of nurseries, capable of producing (eventually) 50 millions of vine branches yearly, from 1 million to 2 million other vine stocks being sold, at a moderate price, from the forest vineyards. In the Department of Horticulture the State possesses 36 nurseries with an area of 940 acres, producing every year 7,000,000 shoots and 50,000 grafted stocks; it has planted 5,600 miles of highways with fruit trees, short courses of lectures on fruit cultivation being given to road surveyors; and it has established drying-kilns, wine-presses and distilleries to encourage the growers to turn to account the fruit they cannot sell fresh." There is also a State poultry-farm, a State bee-farm, intended as models; and it also keeps a silk-worm breeding station "which provides the public with healthy eggs, propagates mulberry trees, and distributes several millions of them every year, and even buys the cocoons from the peasants who have bred the silk-worms, some two dozen State "cocoon-eries" being set up for this purpose.

The cases I have cited above are instances of exceptional State facilities under which any industry is bound to grow and prosper; and it is a matter of regret that the Government of a country, where such or similar facilities are most needed, has been so tardy to recognise their advantages. While it must be conceded that, in the present state of education and enlightenment of the masses in this country such wide and elaborate facilities are neither feasible nor expected, some such ideal as Canada or the United States may be constantly kept in view in order to gradually introduce into India that thorough and intensive system of agriculture which will secure the maximum value and quantity of crops from a given area. The greatest difficulty in the way of a widespread system of agricultural reform is the want of capital. For want of capital the ryots are unable to replenish the land which is being gradually exhausted; for want of capital they are unable to purchase modern and more useful implements, improved seeds and soil fertilisers. A thoroughgoing system of agriculture should aim more specially at the provision of capital for the ryots and the wide diffusion of an elementary general education along certain practical lines, than instruction in the scientific methods at a few centres of education and experiment, which necessarily circumscribes its utility and operation. I suggest below how such a system can be most successfully organised, and how the difficulties about the provision of funds can be overcome.

It cannot, perhaps, be denied that the interest of our landowners in the progress of agriculture is inferior to that of none in India. Indeed, it is vital and supreme. In Bengal there are 916 estates in respect of each of which the landowners pay an annual Government revenue of Rs. 5,000 and upwards. They may be classed as rich landholders. These gentlemen and noblemen have evinced no practical interest in the improvement of their estates beyond what is necessary to prevent them from actual deterioration. If all the zemindars of Bengal could combine for the purpose of starting a few agricultural associations in typical districts—districts widely varying in natural and physical characteristics—and would introduce improved methods of agriculture, on scientific lines, in the estates or portions of estates comprised in those districts, what a glorious vista of prosperity and wealth would open up before many years were over! They have influence, they have leisure, and above all they are in possession of the necessary power to create and promote an associative spirit among their tenants. If these were supplemented by an annual sum commensurate with their incomes, a complete and practical scheme of agricultural association could be inaugurated without difficulty. The British Indian Association of Calcutta, for example, numbers on its rolls some of the richest and most enlightened representatives of the landed aristocracy of the Province. Unfortunately the activities of the Association are confined to political, civic, or commercial topics. In fact it embraces in its functions every conceivable subject of importance and public interest with the exception of just the one in which it is most vitally interested. From motives of self-interest, if not of patriotism, the members may find it advantageous to reconstruct the Association on an economic basis, and make a serious endeavour to improve and develop an industry which, if scientifically conducted, will prove a highly profitable source of investment. Let me illustrate my point by one or two examples. The gross area of the 916 considerable estates is about 40 million acres. If the productive capacity of one acre could be increased by six annas (*i e.*, 2 annas per bigha) the gross wealth of Bengal would be increased by one-and-a-half crores of rupees a year. A larger increment in the productive capacity would, of course, result in a proportionate increase of wealth. Is not this prospect attractive enough to call forth the energy and enterprising spirit of our landlords, and is it too feeble a stimulant to create among them a spirit of co-operation? I hope they will make an experiment: if they succeed, their prosperity and wealth will be the envy and applause of an industrial province; if they fail, the loss will neither be ruinous nor irretrievable. Foreign capital and enterprise have already begun to invade the field of agricultural exploitation; in the Central Provinces European capitalists have taken up the cultivation of *sisal* hemp, and a lease of Government forest land has been granted in the Sambalpur District for that purpose. It behoves the landowners of the country to arrest the progress of the Europeanisation of agriculture, and to prevent foreign capitalists from a participation in the natural wealth of the country which legitimately belongs to her sons.

To give another illustration: in Bengal alone there are 10 millions of acres of cultivable waste other than fallow—or 30 millions of bighas. If these vast areas could be so managed, without destroying the natural forests, that a bigha could yield half a rupee per annum, this would add another crore and-a-half to the wealth of Bengal!

The means by which knowledge of the improved methods of agriculture can be disseminated are unfortunately circumscribed by the peculiar conditions of the country. The foremost factor in this process is co-operation. In Ireland, whose case is almost analogous to that of India, and whose agriculture and domestic industries are the only sources of national wealth, the growth of a spirit of co-operation has achieved remarkably practical and useful results within the last 15 years. The country has emerged from her position of agricultural decadence and of complete subjection to the adverse and malignant influences of foreign competition solely through the development of a national co-operative spirit. The spirit was roused by the economic propaganda spread by a devoted and enthusiastic band of patriots who brought the movement into being. For the moment all party differences were sunk in the earnestness for national reform, and the Nationalists and the Unionists worked with a cordiality rarely found on other occasions. The movement has overcome the obstructive prejudices of the people, their apathy and their suspicions. The organisation of agricultural societies was the next step forward in the salvation of the depressed Irish peasantry. My idea is that the British Indian Association of Calcutta and the Landholders' Association of Bankipore, as Central Boards, should organise an agricultural society in each district, which should enrol as its members the principal cultivating landholders of the locality presided over by the local zemindar or patnidar, or other superior landlord. The functions of the society should be to disseminate, through an itinerant instructor or instructors, advanced ideas of scientific cultivation, illuminated by experiments where necessary. It should advise the people as to the best and most profitable crops—both foreign and indigenous—as to double crops, as to how soils suited to the culture of specially valuable plants may be prepared, how commercial products can be grown, and how gradually agricultural industries may be developed. It should also be its duty to distribute or sell, on the easiest terms, the best quality of seeds and manures, and, so far as funds permit, to keep in stock selected kinds of improved agricultural implements or machinery, both for experimental purposes and for loan to the villagers. It should grant subsidies or rewards for the successful culture of those products which add materially to the national wealth, or solve an economic or industrial difficulty. It should arrange to deliver lectures or give demonstrations in a popular style on the elementary principles of hygiene, domestic economy, thrift, cleanliness, and other subjects of practical usefulness. Under the control and supervision of the society a dairy or a poultry might be established at every important centre of population; and the society might also organise institutions for the promotion of industries connected with agriculture. Under the auspices of the Local or the District Board, the society should hold periodically an agricultural exhibition in which the fullest instruction and information regarding the exhibits should be supplied to the villagers or their representatives. The All-India Agricultural Exhibition, organised by the Indian National Congress, has come to be regarded as an annual "spectacular amusement," and serves no useful purpose in the economy of rural life; whereas the sole and real object of an agricultural exhibition should be to stimulate the active interest of the rural, and not of the urban, population, in the value and use of the exhibits. The Congress Exhibitions are open to a limited class of visitors who can afford to purchase admittance; and their educative influence does not reach the class of people for whom they are specially held. The proposed district exhibitions, to which admittance should be free, ought to stimulate competition for the culture of products for which the soil and climate of the district are specially fitted by nature, or which can be grown by specially scientific methods. No useful purpose is served by holding agricultural exhibitions in industrial centres. It must be remembered that agriculture is a rural, and manufactures are an urban, industry, and the village and the town are respectively favourable for the industry most congenial to each. Besides the above facilities enumerated, others might be extended which would ensure to the ryots success or encouragement in their humble but important occupation. The society should be financed by the State, the District or Local Board, and the zemindar, all of whom should contribute in fair shares.

The above are the bare outlines of a scheme of agricultural improvement which, in my humble view, will be found suitable in this country as a means of increasing the wealth of 65 per cent. of the population who are most liable to famine. There are economists who advocate the growth of manufacturing industries without giving a thought to the improvement of the greatest industry of the country and forget that the former are not absolutely essential for the promotion of national wealth. Denmark is a living example of what agriculture and agricultural industries can achieve in the path of national prosperity. The national wealth per head of population of Denmark is £230, against £247 of England, £224 of France, £216 of Holland, and £165 of Switzerland. In 1893 Denmark exported eggs, butter and bacon to the value of 7 millions; to-day the value is over 15 millions. The remarkable strides which Denmark has made in the manufacture of dairy products ought to furnish an object-lesson to our countrymen of the immense possibilities for the agricultural products of India. The Danish farmer lives a life of great simplicity, contentment and affluence. He has no debts beyond those incurred on the purchase of lands. "The younger men and women are well-dressed, without finery, being neatly and plainly attired in suitable clothes......The women appear to have no desire for silks, ribbons, or feathers; these being considered not only a luxury, but a waste of money, which might be more profitably employed." "Diligence and industry seem to be the keynote to every person's work—with the housewife, cleanliness, order and comfort for her husband and family seemed to be her object." "The highest in the land are proud to associate with the humblest artizan or farm labourer in the consciousness that the outcome of such association will be to strengthen the intellectual energies of the nation, and elevate the wealth-producer's conception of the duties and responsibilities of citizenship." No poverty exists in the country—poverty which comes in the train of manufacturing industries replacing hand-power by steam and electric power; but there are a few cases of honest poverty in the towns. From this description, Denmark appears to us to be a little paradise of health, wealth and contentment set in our mundane earth. It exemplifies the remarkable fact that agriculture is capable of enriching a country in the same way as industries, without producing the evils of industrialisation, *viz.*, the poverty of the unemployed, the vices and miseries of factory life, the deceits and trickeries of trade, the greed and the luxuries of civilisation. Rural life is full of simplicity and healthy employment, and is free from turmoils and complexities, the battle and struggle of a ruthless and strenuous competition. In a rural community there is wealth without greed, there is health without its demoralising luxuries, there is peace without idleness, there is contentment without want. If India were administered on these lines, she could be as happy, as wealthy and as contented as Denmark.

India cannot afford, without seriously compromising her predominant interests, to suffer her agriculture to fall into neglect and decay, in the same way as Great Britain, which, in pursuance of the doctrine of Cobden, sowed the seeds of the ultimate ruin of her agriculture in order to protect her industries and expand her foreign commerce. The Tariff Commission have shown that up to 1884 the net result of British policy in favour of the free importation of food had been "to make the country dependent on foreign sources for its food-supply, without securing lower prices for consumers. In other words, the prices of wheat, when 65 per cent. of the requirements was imported, was the same as when only 4 per cent. was imported. Moreover, the process was necessarily accompanied by the depopulation of the rural districts, the sacrifice of generations of improvement, the destruction of agricultural capital, and the loss of an immense number of subsidiary industries.'' Since 1871—75 the area under corn has diminished from 11½ million acres to 8⅓ millions, or by about 26 per cent. The yield of wheat has fallen off during the same period from 94 to 52 million bushels, *i.e.*, by about 45 per cent. The poorer class of soils has been gradually abandoned, and "there took place a gradual but an increasing displacement of agriculture by manufacture, a change which is reflected in their rapidly diminishing number of persons engaged in the former." The number of persons, male and female, engaged in agriculture, declined within the last 50 years by about 1,200,000; and since 1885, the value of the imports of foodstuffs of all kinds has increased by 80 millions of pounds sterling. These are the mournful results of the *laisser-faire* policy of Great Britain, which it would be dangerous to adopt in India. If India ever comes down from her agricultural eminence, she will have no world-wide industry to fall back upon as her national support; and I doubt very much if Great Britain will come to her rescue if such a moment in her economic existence ever arrives.

Large manufacturing industries not a suitable remedy for India.

I believe, and firmly too, that India's economic salvation, so far as the 200 millions of her agricultural population are concerned, is to be sought not in large manufacturing industries but (1) in the development of agriculture and agricultural industries; and (2) in the resuscitation of her indigenous arts and industries. The economic theory that the successful competition of India with formidable industrial rivals is possible at all times and under all circumstances, is the dream of enthusiastic patriots. It must not be forgotten that the industrial prosperity of Great Britain is the result of a combination of physical, moral and political circumstances which have not been witnessed in the history of India. "The most casual traveller through England to-day," writes Mr. Cunningham, "could hardly fail to remark that a very large part of national industry is concentrated in the northern counties . . . These northern counties, where water-power, as well as coal and iron, is to be found, have attracted to them the textile industries for which they afford both mechanism and power on the easiest terms . . Political, moral, and industrial changes are closely interconnected and react on one another . . . Political views not only control the application of national wealth, but affect its increase. Industrial progress has often been stimulated by new political aims and conditions. Changes in the constitution of society, and in the policy and foreign relations of the country, have given an altered frame-work to which our industry and commerce have, time after time, been forced to adapt themselves. The marriage of Edward III with Philippa, the severities of Alba, the revocation of the Edict of Nantes had conspicuous results in England; the aims of the Angevins to set our towns free to carry on a prosperous trade; the ambition of later days led to the formation of our colonists and the successful struggle for mercantile supremacy . . . Our national policy is not the direct outcome of our economic conditions; whereas, time after time, our industrial life has been directly and permanently affected by political affairs—and politics are more important than economics in English History."

The climatic and physical characteristics of Great Britain have no less influenced her industries than politics. They are one of the determining factors of the conditions of labour. The inhabitants of a temperate country, where the necessaries of life cannot be procured without strenuous effort, and sometimes by conflict with nature, must be possessed of energy, power of endurance, and vigour of mind, which are not the indispensable qualifications of the inhabitants of a country provided with natural plenty. The insular position of Great Britain has endowed the race with a hardihood, a power of resistance, and independence which cannot be easily acquired by a people living under enervating influences. The physical and political conditions which have moulded the British nation and imparted a vigour and vitality to its industry are entirely different from those prevailing in India. The greatest disadvantage, however, under which India labours at present is her fiscal and commercial dependence. The whole tariff policy of India is guided and controlled by His Majesty's Government which is the final arbiter of her commercial destiny. Trade and commerce are the dominating factors in the policy of British administration which is influenced to a large extent by the mercantile school of politicians at home. The Government of India have no voice in the commercial relations of the mother country and her great dependency, far less in formulating an independent commercial policy best suited to the interests of India. "Measures affecting the tariff touch subjects which are not exclusively an Indian concern," wrote Lord Salisbury to Lord Northbrook in 1876. "They influence," His Lordship continued, "the prosperity of trade and industry outside the confines of India, and they relate to matters on which His Majesty's Government is in constant negotiation with foreign powers. Such considerations may furnish important elements in considering the expediency of financial proposals, but they are necessarily less fully within the cognisance of the Indian than of the Imperial Government." The attitude of the foreign countries towards India in the matter of tariff policy is no less suicidal to Indian interests. They have built up large and profitable industries by imposing discriminating duties on Indian products. The whole trend of this policy is to handicap the progress of India by taxing her manufactured products. How far Great Britain will consent to modify this selfish and narrow policy remains to be seen. But the time is yet far distant when the foreign countries will acquiesce in its modification in a manner which, according to their accepted policy, will prejudice their industries and favour those of India. Neither is the attitude of the British Government entirely free from all blemishes of suspicion. The Government of India have, of late, denounced the so-called *swadeshi* movement, and have promulgated various orders and resolutions for the development of what they style "honest" *swadeshi*. They have freely countenanced the growth of joint-stock enterprise, the establishment of technical schools and colleges, and the efforts of private individuals and associations to give Indians a foreign education in various branches of technical instruction. But I ask if all these professions are sincere; and if they are sincere now, will they remain so to the bitter end. Those who have watched the trend of British politics in India during the last 50 years must have observed that official sympathy, official aid, and official favours have emanated from a Government possessed of a pronounced sense of superiority of the rulers over the ruled. Fifty years ago, a big chasm separated them in respect of education, self-respect and other characteristics of manhood. Official relations between the governing classes and the governed were then more cordial, official favours more profuse, and official sympathy more conspicuous. The chasm is now being slowly filled up, and the two parties are approaching each other in a spirit of healthy rivalry. This spirit is intolerable to a race which has dominated the mind and intellect of their subjects for the last century-and-a-half. If a subject race does not meekly submit to the moral and physical force of the ruling race, or acknowledge its superiority, the situation engendered thereby is called a political crisis; and such a crisis has now arisen. While a similar crisis in economic life is yet far off, signs of its birth are in evidence. Fifty years ago the Government advocated education, and anticipated with glory and delight the advent of a period of political renaissance and the growth of political aspirations among the people of India. When that period actually arrived, it brought with it regrets and disappointments. Fifty years hence our rulers, however enthusiastic in their support of genuine *swadeshi* they may be now, will not behold with equanimity a situation in which their own interests bid fair to be jeopardised by reason of Great Britain's rivalry with India. Self-interest will then get the better of her moral obligations towards India, and she will not hesitate to extinguish honest *swadeshi* by all means in her power, military or legislative, if it will grow strong and vigorous enough to threaten or imperil her trade in the Indian market. It is evident, therefore, that unless India attains a fiscal and political autonomy, her industrial and commercial progress must necessarily be very slow. English colonies as well as all foreign countries, with which Indian trade is gradually increasing, are slowly building up protective tariff walls against the importation of Indian, British and foreign manufactures. The day is far distant when these countries will regard the interests of India as superior to theirs, and allow the Indian manufacturing industries to thrive at the expense of their own. An autonomous fiscal policy is the only weapon by which India can successfully compete with her industrial rivals, but alas for the day when India will be empowered to negotiate with the Powers in her own interests! For some long time to come India must perfect her agriculture, increase her agricultural products, and export raw materials. If there is any manufacturing industry in which she can compete with foreigners it is the manufacture of jute and cotton, leather and sugar, of which there is an unlimited demand for home consumption.

The Industrial prosperity of Germany is the result of environment—of the inevitable struggle for national supremacy carried on under circumstances highly favourable to success. The progress of Germany may be dated from the termination of the Franco-German War in 1871, when she received the French war indemnity of two hundred million pounds sterling. This gave her a splendid capital to start with in her subsequent uninterrupted career of progress; for, the whole amount was expended, under the most sagacious advice, on various works of public and administrative improvements, and the Government was enabled, with the help of the national revenues, set free in this manner, to direct its funds, its energy, and its intellect, to the organisation and development of an extensive and thoroughgoing scheme of industrial and technical education. The protective policy of 1879 is no less responsible for her national progress. "The duties were high enough to confer a distinct benefit on the products of national industries and agriculture in competing with similar products from abroad. They were not, however, placed at such a level as to impede the producer's natural ability or to prevent his keeping the cost of production and all other expenses connected with an energetic competition for the markets of the world, as low as possible. Since that time the Imperial Government have always followed the principle of not only affording a struggling industry initial, but also continuous, protection afterwards, whenever foreign competition materially threatened its prospects. The protective system appears to have been favourable to a rapid expansion of foreign trade." The result of this policy, which has been wisely and steadfastly pursued for the last thirty years, is the industrial supremacy of Germany, of which we have so much evidence to-day. Can India successfully compete with Germany under these circumstances? I must answer emphatically in the negative.

The case of Japan is similar. The country, homogeneous, as it is, in language, in religion and in national sentiment, became suddenly, as it were, awakened to a sense of its national importance. It enjoyed the political advantages of a free government, which directed its fiscal and commercial policy along healthy channels, controlled its education, and encouraged the development of national spirit, vigour and morality. As a result we see the Japan of to-day emerging as the rival of the European powers. Are the conditions of India analogous, and can the present political and social conditions of India produce similar results? I must again answer with an emphatic *no*. It can hardly be expected that in her present social and political condition the industrial spirit of India will be roused to such activity that she will be able to overtake the great rivals in the race. It must never be overlooked that famines in this country mainly affect the agriculturists, numbering about 200 millions of souls; and that the most effective way to conduce to their wealth and prosperity is to foster and develop an industry which concerns this mass. Manufacturing industries, when carried to the highest pitch of progress, can, at best, improve the condition of a million or two of the people; but the remainder, 198 millions of agriculturists, will not be benefited at all. To reach the desired end, the greatest good of the greatest number,—India should place before her as her ideal the agricultural systems of Canada, New Zealand, France, Denmark or the United States. If I may be permitted to hazard an opinion, the power and greatness of the United States consist not so much in her wonderful scientific achievements and their applications to the daily uses of life, as to the command she holds over other countries—especially the United Kingdom—as a great purveyor of their food-supply. (See App. G and H.) Great Britain is a power indeed; but recent experience has shown that in spite of her command over an almost unlimited resource of wealth, she is suffering from an inherent weakness brought on by her dependence on other countries for nearly three-fourths of her food-requirements. She at last realised the grave situation engendered by this perpetual state of dependence, specially in time of war, and a Royal Commission, with Lord Balfour of Burleigh as Chairman, was appointed in January 1904 to investigate the subject and suggest remedies. The Commission, while admitting the gravity of the situation, rely on the faithful observance of the rules of International Law, and on the variety of the sources from which the food-supply of the country is drawn. They also admit that a rise in the price of wheat is inevitable, which will, of course, result in an economy of consumption and in the use of its substitutes. They regard, however, with grave concern, the effect of this rise—which may be very high on account of the war panic—on the condition of the poorer classes who will be the first to feel the pinch. The poorer classes, who will be actually affected, number 12 millions out of 42; and the economic effect will not be so slight as is assumed to be. A number of remedies are suggested to ensure a sufficient stock of food in the country in times of panic and danger but this, in my opinion, is the least important part of the Report. With all deference to the optimistic views held by the Commission, the danger of the position, which has been clearly pointed out and repeatedly brought home by publicists and economists, cannot be wholly ignored. A strong sense of alarm and danger pervades the Report, and however skilfully one may try to belittle them, they cannot be wholly disregarded. Here, then, is an example which should not be without its lessons in India. She cannot afford to buy food from over the seas for her poor population, whose wealth and prosperity must, for all time to come, depend on the value in the market of the surplus produce of the land. If this surplus showed any signs of shrinkage in pursuance of the short-sighted policy of fostering industry at the cost of agriculture, and of diverting the agriculturists from their industrious and healthy rural pursuits to factory life in towns, the country will be exposed to all the evils of modern industrialism which our countrymen can imagine. The proportion of the poor to the rich and middle-class in India is exactly the reverse of what it is in the United Kingdom. The food production of the country must, therefore, be of such magnitude as will not only be sufficient to feed without cost her own producers as well as a portion of the population of the mother country, but to pay her foreign obligations, and at the same time put some cash into their pockets to enable them to purchase a few imported necessaries of life.

The more the purchasing power of the people is increased by this means, the greater will it contribute to the taxation of the country, and the more will the individual and the nation rise in the scale of material wealth. Moreover, the soil and climate of India, no less than the habits of the people and the cost of production, are eminently favourable to the successful competition in agriculture with foreigners. There appear to me to be more glorious possibilities for India in the improvement of her agriculture than in the formation of new and costly industrial organisations. If the productive capacity of an acre of cultivated land could be increased in money-value by six annas—which is not absolutely impossible under a scientific and intensive method—the agricultural wealth of the country could be increased by about 9 crores of rupees a year. This is equivalent to interest at 5 per cent. on a capital investment of 180 crores of rupees. How long and difficult will it be before the co-operation of the entire population of British Indian Empire can produce an association of capital so gigantic in magnitude as this for the purpose of promoting industrial capitalism ? And is there any hope of increasing the national wealth by nine crores a year by means of any industrial organisations that we can at present think of ? Yet how easy and practicable it seems to enhance the yield per bigha by only two annas ! In the Report of the United States Department of Agriculture for 1904 the Secretary speaks of the farm products of the country as "unthinkable aggregates." It is with pride and gratification in the consciousness of the superiority of agriculture to industry that he writes: "An occupation that has produced such an unthinkable value as one aggregating five billion dollars within a year may be better measured by some comparisons. All the gold-mines of the entire world have not produced, since Columbus discovered America, a greater value of gold than the farmers of this country have produced in wealth in two years ; this year's product is over six times the amount of the capital stock of all national banks; it comes within three-fourths of a billion dollars of equalling the value of the manufactures of 1900, less the cost of materials used; it is twice the sum of our exports and imports for a year; it is two-and-a-half times the gross earnings from the operations of the railways; it is three-and-a-half times the value of all minerals produced in the country, including coal, iron-ore, gold, silver, and quarried stone." I can easily conceive that agriculture is capable of producing similar results in India if those that are interested in land will co-operate for its improvement.

The industries suited to Indian habits of life are those that provide employment for the largest number of artizans and handicraftsmen in their respective spheres of hereditary occupations. Steam and electric-power factories provide occupation for a particular class of labour; but there exists in the country a vast mass of industrious poor, including women, whose lot can never be improved by the multiplication of mills and factories, because they consider it degrading to work side by side with the lowest class of professional labourers. It is desirable to harness the energies of this class of people, that are at present running to waste, and to turn them into profitable use in the labour market. The industries in which they can be advantageously employed are mostly manual industries carried on in the homes of the artizans, and are generally known as cottage or indigenous industries. The greatest patriot of India is he who, by his knowledge, experience, energy, and power of co-operation, will succeed in improving existing industries, or to galvanise into life the moribund ones. It is needless to give a complete catalogue of the different kinds of indigenous industries pursued in the different parts of India; but the following may be cited as the most important: the weaving of Bengal and Madras; the stone-carving of Orissa, Rajputana, the United Provinces, and Central India; the ivory-carving of Murshidabad, Delhi, Mysore and Burma; the silk manufactures of Murshidabad, Assam, Kashmir and Benares; the gold and silver filigree work of Orissa and Dacca; the wood-carving of Mysore, Bombay, Burma and the Punjab; the carpet manufacture of Mirzapore; the painted-ware of Jaipur, Delhi, Lucknow and Benares; the inlaid marble work of Agra; and the pottery work of various places in India. These productions of art have always won the admiration of the civilised world, but they are gradually falling in popular favour, and are sometimes being supplanted by the cheap, machine-made imitations from Europe. The chief difficulty connected with their development is to find a market. The fashion of the country has undergone a decided change, whether for the better or for the worse we cannot judge. Our nobility and gentry have no longer a taste for our world-famed Kashmir shawls and the Dacca muslins; they prefer Western style both in their social and domestic life. The purchasing capacity of the middle and lower classes, unless the articles wanted are necessaries or moderate luxuries, does not count for much in the market. The problem therefore is how to revive the old taste; and it is not, I believe, incapable of solution. If a powerful central organisation could be formed for the advertisement of the art-wares, having branches in different parts of the country affiliated to it, the love of the people for the productions of

Revival of cottage or domestic industries—a remedy.

their own country bids fair to be revived by a persistent and powerful appeal to their taste. But I admit that this requires a fund of energy, enterprise, and capital which our patriots and country-men cannot easily command. For the present, therefore, we must be content with the admirable work which the "Indian Stores" and similar other smaller institutions are doing on a humble scale in this particular field of action. The "Indian Stores" has proved a highly profitable concern, and it is surprising that strong motives of gain do not bring out capital from the hoards of the rich for the purpose of being invested in similar concerns which are at once productive and patriotic.

Improvement of mino handicrafts—a remedy.

Besides the arts mentioned above, in which skilled labour is necessary, there are various minor occupations and handicrafts which are at present carried on with no particular intelligence and skill. Among these may be mentioned, as the most common,—gardening, carpentry and joinery, straw-plaiting, basket-making, tailoring, hosiery, masonry, shoe-making, needlework, lace-making, embroidery, millinery, dress-making, bookbinding, packing, modelling in clay or wood, cutlery, smithery, etc. A complete list will be found in Appendix F. An immense improvement can be effected in these minor branches of industry by what is called "technical education." I use the expression in the sense in which Professor Perry has used it, *viz.*, "an education in the scientific and artistic principles which govern the occupations in any industry. It is neither a science nor an art, nor the teaching of a handicraft. It is that without which a master is an unskilful master, a workman is an unskilled workman, a clerk or a farmer, an unskilled clerk or a farmer." It implies, in its simplest significance, the application of intelligence, skill and commonsense by which a manufacturer is enabled to produce works of better style, finish and symmetry, and therefore of higher beauty, usefulness and value. It is quite possible by the application of such technical knowledge to adapt the products to the varying fashions and requirements of the times, and to attract more extensive patronage. This technical knowledge should be applied to every variety of article in daily use, the production of which makes the producer a useful member of society in his own particular line of occupation. There is an urgent and most pressing need in India for this kind of elementary technical instruction by which a carpenter may be a skilled carpenter, a blacksmith may be a skilled blacksmith, and a gardener, a skilled gardener. The amelioration of this class of petty handicraftsmen, is the second step towards the advancement of the scheme for the prevention of famine among a considerable body of labourers who constitute, numerically, a class next in importance to the agriculturists in this country. To carry out this scheme, I suggest the establishment of a technical school in every district, under the patronage of our wealthy men, to be maintained by the joint aid of the State, the District and Municipal Boards, and designed to impart elementary practical instruction in as many branches of the parochial industries as are suited to the aptitudes and preoccupations of the villagers, or calculated to supply local needs, or to cater for the popular taste. A general spread of elementary technical knowledge of this description will gradually help to supersede crude and unskilled methods of manufacture, improve the quality of workmanship, attract greater patronage of the people, enhance the value of the products, and ultimately redound to the advantage of the manufacturer. No costly organisation seems to be necessary. A district technical school of modest proportions can be established at an initial cost of Rs. 1,000 and a recurring annual expenditure of Rs. 2,400. This small charge may be apportioned between the Government, the Local or Municipal Board, and the local wealthy people, in certain reasonable shares.

I have stated above that the most effective remedies for raising 200 millions of people above distress and poverty at the time of famine, are (1) to encourage and develop agriculture and agricultural industries in preference to manufacturing industries; (2) to promote indigenous or cottage industries (including, of course, weaving and spinning); and (3) to employ skill, intelligence and commonsense to improve the workmanship of a certain class of petty industries from which a large class of day-labourers derive their livelihood. In respect of the first remedy, I have suggested the establishment of district associations in each district, and in the next section I will indicate how the cost of these associations can be met. As regards the second remedy, it has often been argued that hand-power cannot compete successfully with steam or electric-power; but this argument is not of much practical value when we consider the very cheap labour employed in this country, and the fact that some of the industries have still survived the unfavourable and unequal competition with industries carried on by mechanical power. On this point I cannot refrain from quoting the sound and wise observations made by a gentleman who now occupies a high position in the Indian administration: "It is not a law of nature," says he, "that steam-power should supersede hand-power; it has been the consequence only of the special conditions of Europe, where the power required is not in excess of that which can be supplied by the human body; it is a calculation of the relative cost which decides whether steam-power or hand-power shall be applied to manufacture. Hand-power is expensive in the west of Europe, and manufacturers, therefore, are constantly striving to replace it by steam-power; but in India, at the present day, hand-power is cheap, and is generally more economical (to the employer) than steam-power. . . . . If, therefore, the efficiency of the hand-power industries in India could be very considerably increased, it is probable that they would be able to compete successfully with the steam-power industries of Europe." As regards the third remedy, I will deal with the matter in the next section, which deals with the financial aspect of the question.

Financial remedies.

The question of the provision of funds for the reforms I have outlined above is the most important factor in the scheme. To remove the difficulty I would reconstitute the "Famine Insurance Grant" on a wider, a sounder, and more practical basis. To explain the nature of this grant, which now stands at 150 lakhs of rupees, I cannot do better than to recall to mind the memorable speech of Sir John Strachey, delivered in Lord Lytton's Council on the 27th of December 1877, defining the scope and object of the grant. "I reminded the Council," said he, ". . . . that after the famine of 1874 in Northern Bengal, the Government of Lord Northbrook declared that such calamities could no longer be treated as abnormal or exceptional, and that sound financial principles required that the grave obligations entailed by famine upon the Government should be explicitly recognised and provided for among the ordinary charges of the State. Within the previous ten years three serious famines had occurred . . . . As it could not be doubted that India was liable to the periodical and not infrequent occurrence of such calamities, Lord Northbrook most justly concluded that to attempt to meet them merely by borrowing without a simultaneous increase of income would be financially ruinous; it was out of the question to think of meeting, with borrowed money, the charges which we should have to incur in future on their account. Whatever means we may take to obviate or mitigate them, it must, under present circumstances, be looked upon as inevitable that famines will, from time to time, occur. He therefore determined that to enable the State to meet the serious obligation of *preventing* and relieving famine, it was necessary to secure, in prosperous times, a substantial surplus of revenue over expenditure in addition to that necessary margin which a prudent administration demands for the ordinary requirements of the State. Due provision would thus be made to meet occasional expenditure upon famine. . . . I am not able to compute with certainty the cost of the famine of 1866 in Orissa; but it has been estimated at £1,700,000 (170 lakhs of rupees). . . . . Even as regards the Bengal famine of 1874, and the famine in Southern India of 1876 and 1877, it will be obvious, on reflection, that it must be long before the accounts of receipts and expenditure can be completed. . . . . The extra expenditure in consequence of famine upon the several services . . . . may be more precisely ascertained. On the other hand, the revenue lost under many heads of accounts, and the net revenue gained upon the railways, although real and important elements in the accounts of a famine, can never be exactly known. Without troubling the Council with further details, I have said enough to show that the actual cost of a famine must, to the end, be the subject of estimate rather than of accounts. The Bengal famine of 1874 is, in this way, estimated to have cost £6,750,000 (675 lakhs), and the famine in Southern India . . . . is now estimated to cost £9 250,000* (925 lakhs) making a charge of £16,000,000 (16 crores) for famine relief in the five years from 1873 to 1878. Making all allowances for these considerations, I cannot now venture to estimate the yearly *cost of famines in loss of revenue and actual expenditure* at less than £1,500,000. This amount has necessarily been arrived at in a somewhat arbitrary manner, and it will be seen to correspond approximately with the sum that would be requisite to distribute the charges of the last five years over a period of ten years. *It will remain for the Government in the future, to reconsider, from time to time, the practical result of the assumption which we are now constrained to make, on what are necessarily imperfect grounds, and to take all requisite steps in the way of correcting any error into which further experience may indicate that we have fallen, either in the one direction or in the other.*" The italics are mine. It will be seen from the above lengthy extract, which explains clearly the policy underlying this much-debated grant, that the avowed object of the Government of India was to fix the grant at 150 lakhs subject to modification in the light of later experience, the criterion for determining the grant being the extent to which the aggregate surpluses of the years were affected by the loss of revenue and increase of expenditure due to famines. Since the standard grant of 150 lakhs was fixed 30 years ago, the recurrence of famines has become more frequent, their extent has become wider, their intensity more severe, and their financial and economic effects more disastrous. If we were called

---

* According to a later estimate the cost was 11¼ millions (see footnote at page 40 of the Report of the Royal Commission on Indian Expenditure).

upon to fix a grant now, we should embrace in our calculation the decennial period commencing with 1895-96, and estimate, as the basis of the grant, the cost of the famines for this and the succeeding nine years. The total direct famine-relief expenditure during this period has amounted to nearly 18 crores, and the total indirect expenditure and loss of revenue has run up to 13 crores. The aggregate surpluses of these ten years have, therefore, been affected by a sum of 31 crores, or by 3 crores on an average every year, against an average of 1½ crores tentatively adopted by Sir John Strachey in 1878. The effects of the recent appalling calamities have revolutionized the financial administration of famines in India; and in view of the definite declaration that the amount of the grant should be open to revision, it is the duty of the Government now to consider whether the economic conditions of India do not justify a provision of 3 crores being made annually to give complete effect to the policy of 1877. The taxation of the Indian population at the present time, cannot be characterised as excessive; and the proposed increase of grant can be easily provided out of the current revenues without recourse to further taxation. I would prefer an annual expenditure of 1½ crores on the material and intellectual well-being of the people to a relief of taxation by that amount. It will perhaps be contended that to provide out of taxation an increased grant under "Famine Relief and Insurance" will be an unsound economic policy; but if the grant is earmarked to finance the agriculturists with the ultimate object of improving the productiveness of the land, and thereby raising their material condition, no ampler justification can be found for a better and a surer form of famine insurance. The prosecution of protective railways has been carried on at a too rapid rate, and the necessity for further protective railways may be said to have altogether ceased. It would, I consider, be a more prudent course if the Government were to abandon their traditional ideas of financial orthodoxy by devoting one-half of the proposed three crores grant to finance the agriculturists. The objects which appear to me directly conducive to their welfare are: the purchase of superior qualities of seed, improved agricultural implements, seeds of valuable exotic plants suited to the soil and climate of India, purchase of natural and artificial fertilisers, purchase of cuttings, bulbs, plants—foreign and indigenous—loans and grants for land improvement, etc. A share of the cost of the district agricultural associations might also be met from the 3 crores grant. There are about 250 districts in the whole of British India, and if we assume that we have one association in each district, there will be about 250 associations in the whole country. The average monthly cost of each association may be taken to be Rs. 5,000, including grants and subsidies to the agriculturists, the pay of the itinerant instructors, the cost of the exhibitions, etc. The total annual cost of 250 district associations would, therefore, be a crore-and-a-half. Of this sum 100 lakhs might be provided by the Government, 75 of which will come out of the reconstituted Famine Grant, and 25 out of the normal grant under "Scientific and other Minor Departments." The balance 50 lakhs might be divided between the Zemindars and local bodies in the ratio of their respective capacities. The ordinary income of all mofussil municipalities is about 250 lakhs, and of the District and Local Boards about 400 lakhs—total 650 lakhs. A contribution of 5 per cent. on their income by these local bodies would produce an annual income of 32½ lakhs. The balance 17½ lakhs may reasonably be contributed by Zemindars and other private individuals.

The second source on which the funds required for financing the agriculturists might be drawn is the deposits in the Post Office Savings Banks. The idea may at first sound as revolutionary, but it is not altogether novel. In Italy the earnings of town industry, deposited in the savings banks, are utilised for the benefit of the rural industries. There is nothing financially objectionable in this method, for agriculture ultimately benefits the urban industries. In India, the savings bank balances are merged in the general cash balance of the Government, and are partly drawn upon for the construction of productive public works. The investment of a portion of these trust funds on public works is undoubtedly profitable to the Government, as it obviates the necessity of the public debt to the extent of the available surplus. If a modicum of this surplus is utilised annually to finance the agriculturists, it will merely reduce railway expenditure by that amount, which the country can afford to dispense with under present circumstances. It would not perhaps be difficult or impossible to find, out of the two sources indicated above, 2½ crores of rupees annually which will go a great way towards solving the preliminary financial difficulties connected with the scheme of famine insurance or famine-prevention.

A great development of agriculture may be stimulated through the agency of Local and Municipal Boards in this country. It will, perhaps, be urged that local bodies have no interest in rural industries carried on outside their legal jurisdiction, and that agriculture is, therefore, not a proper object of local fund expenditure. It will, however, be remembered that the trades and industries of urban centres are mostly dependent on raw produce, and a decline or temporary failure of agricultural products is inevitably followed by depression of trade. In the United States report of agriculture for 1902 I find the following passage which bears on this subject: "Since successful agriculture is essential to the prosperity and well-being of urban as well as rural communities, there should be co-operation between country districts, villages, cities, and the States to provide the means for the maintenance of agricultural courses in the high schools." If land is not in a healthy and fertile condition, it is evident that labour and capital alone cannot create or reproduce national wealth. The three factors must combine and work together. I am therefore unable to accept the force of the argument that local bodies have no interest in, and local funds cannot legitimately be diverted to, agricultural improvement. The Government should accordingly take steps to enable our local bodies to subsidise and support agriculture and agricultural instruction as a primary object of local funds. The Bengal Local Self-Government Act is now in course of revision, and the Bengal Government should take the opportunity to insert the necessary clause in the Bill.

APPENDICES.

APPENDIX A.

Extracts from Col. Baird Smith's Report on the Famine of 1860-61.

Para. 36.—. . . . To my own mind I confess it appears clear that no misapprehension can be greater than to suppose that the settlement of the public demand on the land is only lightly, or as some say, not at all, connected with the occurrence of famines. It lies in reality far nearer to the root of the matter, because of its intimate and vital relation to the every-day life of the people, and to their growth towards prosperity or towards degradation, than any such accessories as canals, or roads, or the like, important though they unquestionably are. It is no doubt quite true that not the best settlement system which mortal intellect could devise would cover the skies with clouds, or moisten the earth with rain, when the course of nature had established a drought. But given the drought and its consequences, the capacity of the people to resist their destructive influences is in direct proportion—I would almost say geometrical proportion—to the perfection of the settlement system under which they are living and growing.

Para. 62.—Such, then, having been the general results of the protracted fixity of the public demand, the security of titles, the general moderation of assessment, the recognition and careful record of rights, and the reasonably equable distribution of the burden of land taxation, which were the main characteristics of the settlement of 1833—45, the inference seems irresistible that to intensify and perpetuate these results we must proceed still farther in the same healthy and fruitful direction. The good which has been done by partial action on sound principles is both a justification and encouragement to further advances, and entertaining the most earnest conviction that State interests and popular interests would be alike strengthened in an increasing ratio by this step. The first, and as I believe, the most important remedial measure I have respectfully to submit for consideration is the expediency of fixing for ever the public demand on the land, and thus converting the existing settlements in the first great subdivisional section of the tract of country now under reference from settlements for long periods into settlements for perpetuity. I limit this to the first subdivision at present simply for convenience. The second subdivision is much mixed and still, in part at least, in a state of transition, unsuited to the adoption of the course which can safely be recommended for the first. But if it should hereafter appear that the same principle can be extended beyond the limits of the first subdivision . . . . its beneficial influence would there be the same.

Para. 64.—It may be supposed that a great sacrifice of public revenue is involved in the conversion of a perpetually fixed demand on the part of Government. It is to be observed, however, that (with a single exception to be noticed separately) the recent tendency of the measures of Government has shown a different conviction and indicated a belief that its interests are best secured not by general enhancement but by a general lightening of its demand on land. The latest orders under which settlements now in progress are conducted prescribe a reduction of the proportion of the rent or the net produce, hitherto appropriated as Government revenue, from 66 to 50 per cent. ; and I have no doubt that is a most wise and prudent step, sure to justify itself before many years pass away. It is scarcely possible, indeed, that a tax on rent which, even at its minimum, absorbs half that product and presses exclusively on a single section of the community, can be permitted to increase. The tendency will, I believe, be quite in the opposite direction; and, instead of desiring to raise the moderately assessed districts to the level of the highest, the best revenue authorities will probably seek to lighten the pressure on the latter, and in this manner, rather than by the converse process, to equalise the burden generally. Such an equalisation would lead to a universal increase in the wealth of the agricultural classes. The price of land would rise gradually from four or five years' purchase of the Government revenue to ten or twelve times that standard. Capital would, in time, accumulate in other hands than those of money-lenders, or the scarcely taxed native commercial classes in general. The land would enjoy the benefit of such accumulations, and as a necessary consequence of the increased prosperity of that class, which must always be the very core of native society, and with the strength or the weakness of which the social fabric, generally, must always have the acutest sympathy, trade and commerce and general wealth would not only increase, but, as years passed on, the community must grow stronger and stronger, and the risk of its collapsing under any such calamities as that we are now considering would gradually become less and less. Assuming, then, that the results of the measure would, in some degree at any rate, realise these anticipations, it seems unreasonable to suppose that an intelligent and powerful Government could fail to participate in them. Its intelligence would direct it to the least offensive and most effective means of sharing in the general prosperity, and its power would insure the fair trial and ultimate success of those means. There would be no real sacrifice, therefore, I believe, but, on the contrary, a marked increase of public resources from the creation of the increased private prosperity to which it is conceived that a perpetual settlement of the public demand must lead.

Para. 79.—It will be understood, then, that in advocating a perpetual settlement of the public demand on the land as a means of strength and growth to the community in the famine tracts, I contemplate no interference whatever with the existing rights of the soil. The full enjoyment of these *is guaranteed to their proprietors by the most solemn and repeated sanctions.* But I anticipate that under the free action of the laws which mould and form societies, much, if not all that is obstructive and objectionable in the influence of those rights, will gradually disappear. The steady gravitation of capital to the land, of which the evidences are already unquestionable; the tendency to aggregation rather than to minute subdivision of the soil of which proofs are discernible; the growth of wealthy communities such as I have indicated in speaking of the influences of canal irrigation, with many other points,—all indicate the direction in which society is moving; and I am sure that, such being the case, the safest and best policy as regards its internal action is simply to leave it alone, and let it assume its natural forms and conditions, with the smallest amount of external interference that is consistent with good and efficient administration. Sudden or magical strides in improvement are neither expected from fixity of demand nor are they possible. But that the principle is sound and its action satisfactory have been proved by thirty years of trial. The time for the next step in advance is therefore now believed to have arrived; and what is expected from its adoption is only an acceleration of that growth and progress of which, I believe, I have given sufficient proof, and a steady, though more rapid, strengthening of the community in its most vital relations to resist such calamities as have already swept over it, and must be expected to sweep over it again.

Extract from a Minute by the Hon. Mr. E. Maltby, dated the 24th December, 1861.

I am strongly in favour of a permanent assessment for the following reasons: (1) Experience has clearly shown that the great essentials to the prosperity of the ryots are a moderate and fixed assessment, security of possession, and freedom from all interference or annoyance on the part of the native revenue servants, by declaring that so long as they pay a known demand, and no more, they cannot be molested. This end will not be attained if fluctuations of price can enhance Government demand, specially when the means of ascertaining those fluctuations are so imperfect.

Extract from a Minute by the Hon. Mr. Cecil Beadon, dated the 13*th March*, 1862.

In this way, without making any undue sacrifice of its land-revenue, which even now perhaps forms more than a fair or safe proportion of the imperial income, we should confer upon the whole of India the inestimable boon of a fixed settlement, fraught with all the advantages which Bengal has derived from Lord Cornwallis' Settlement, but free from its defects; we should give to every occupant of land the most *powerful inducement that human nature knows to increase the value of his property*, and we should lay the foundation of great and even increasing prosperity, giving wealth and contentment to the people, and security and financial ease to the Government.

Extract from a Minute by the Hon. Mr. Samuel Laing, dated the 7*th April*, 1862.

We do not exist as a Government merely to get the largest revenue we can out of the country, or even to keep the mass of the people in a state of uniform dead level, though it should be a tolerably happy and contented one as a peasant tenantry under a paternal Government.

If we give a permanent settlement, as Mr. Beadon proposes, we lay the foundation for a state of society, not perhaps so easily managed, but far more varied and richer in elements of civilisation and progress. . . . . I have no objection to fix what is now a fair rent for land in cultivation as a permanent rate, and take my chance of getting back, by indirect taxation, whateve revenue I may want owing to a general alteration in money-value arising from the general growth of wealth and prosperity. But I do not think the State should give away, for next to nothing, any considerable mass of land of fair quality, which it is morally certain that a few years of good government and improved communications will bring into cultivation.

Extract from a Minute by Mr. W. Muir, dated the 5th December, 1861.

Looking now to the benefits which may be anticipated in the improvement of property, I notice first the periodical check which the prosperity of the country receives under the present system whenever a settlement approaches near its termination. As the assessment of the coming settlement is to be fixed in reference to the extent of cultivated area and value of the produce, it is the natural object of every proprietor to make these appear as small as possible. Hence, not only is the expenditure of capital on new improvements stayed, but the state of existing prosperity actually depreciated. The proprietor refrains from cultivating the usual breadth of crop; he narrows the area of land under irrigation; he postpones the sowing of valuable staples. It is quite natural that he should do so. The present sacrifice will be amply made up, if even a small diminution of Government demand is thereby obtained. Penalties are threatened for such procedure. But so long as human nature is what it is, penalties will be fruitless, and every fresh settlement upon existing assets will tend to this result.

Leaving out of view the few last years of a temporary settlement, it must be admitted that the effect of a determination of the assessment for 20 or 30 years has been found eminently beneficial in ensuring improvement. Colonel Baird Smith's report bears ample testimony that it is so; almost every district in these provinces is an unequivocal witness to the same truth. The security of a long settlement stimulates industry and encourages the expenditure of capital, for the profits of the period are certain to replace the capital, and to yield a handsome return besides. But it is also certain that the inducements to investing capital in the improvement of the land would, in most cases, be greatly strengthened by fixing the demand in perpetuity. When any large disbursement is now contemplated, it is perfectly natural for the proprietor to hesitate. He will reflect whether it is, after all, worth his while to sink Rs. 1,000, say, in a well which shall add Rs. 200 to his rental, seeing that in consequence of this increased profit he may be sure that at the next settlement Rs. 100 will be added to the assessment of his estate. Had the settlement been permanent, there would, in such a case, have been no doubt about the matter; where the settlement is temporary, the project is, in all likelihood, cast aside.

Extract from a Minute by the Lieut.-Governor of the North-Western Provinces, dated the 27th May, 1862.

I do not in the least doubt that the gradual and cautious concession of a guarantee of permanency to the settlement of land-revenue in the North-Western Provinces, generally, will be productive of all the advantages which Col. Baird Smith and Mr. Muir, in even greater detail, have depicted. Judging by the effects of settlements for long periods, it may be safely anticipated that the limitation of the Government demand in perpetuity will, in a much larger degree, lead to the investment of capital in the land. The wealth of the agricultural classes will be increased. The prosperity of the country and the strength of the community will be augmented. Land will command a much higher price. The prospective loss which the Government will incur by relinquishing its share of the profits, arising from extended cultivation and improved productiveness, will be partly, if not wholly, compensated by the indirect returns which would be derived from the increased wealth and prosperity of the country at large.

Extracts from a Minute by Sir John Lawrence, Bart., G.C.B., K.C.S.I., dated the 5th July, 1862.

I consider that such a measure would produce great practical results, while, if it were not financially beneficial, at any rate it would entail no appreciable loss on the State, and would prove a much greater boon to the mass of the proprietors than the power of redeeming their assessments. While the land-revenue of India is, as I have said, one of the most ancient institutions of that country under all the native governments of which I have any knowledge, it has been more or less a grievous burthen on the agriculturists; and the only mode by which this pressure was alleviated was by special alienations of it, in whole or in part, in favour of particular families or individuals.

* * *

I recommend a perpetual settlement because I am persuaded that, however much the country has of late years improved, its resources will be still more rapidly developed by the limitation of the Government demand. Such a measure will still further encourage the investment of money in the land, and will give still greater security to the land-revenue itself, which in years of great calamity, occurring every now and then, has suffered largely, though the loss has been more or less of a temporary character. It is also very desirable that facilities should exist for the growth of a middle class in India connected with the land, without dispossessing the present yeoman and peasant proprietors. There are many men of much intelligence, spirit and social influence among these classes who are yet so poor that they find it difficult to maintain a decent appearance. It is no remedy for this state of things to confer great and exclusive benefits on a few individuals, specially when these very benefits are conferred at the expense of the rest of the community. What is really wanted is to give the intelligent, the thrifty, and the enterprising among them the opportunity of improving their own condition by the exercise of such qualities; and this can be best done by limiting the public demand on the land. When such men acquire property and are in a thriving state, they are almost certain to be well affected to the Government, and will use their influence, which will generally be considerable, in its favour.

* * *

Further, it may be observed that although it will always be wise to maintain the land-revenue in its integrity as the mainstay of the State, there can be no valid reason why India should not yield a considerable revenue from indirect sources; though it cannot reasonably be hoped that such revenues will suffice to replace the land-revenue if once given up or largely reduced in amount. On the contrary, a moderate and fixed demand on land, by stimulating industry, will gradually but certainly, enable capital to be accumulated, and give the agriculturists the means with which to purchase taxable articles. There can be little doubt that much of the increase which has arisen from such taxation of late years has thus been created. In the Punjab, the general relief which the country obtained by the reduction of the excessive land assessment, and the abolition of the numerous duties in the shape of Octroi, transit duties, and import and export duties, enabled the people to pay an additional excise on salt. The income from that one source of revenue gradually increased from about £40,000 per annum in 1848 to upwards of £200,000 in 1858; while the duty itself was only raised 25 per cent., *viz.*, from 3*s*. on the maund of 80 lbs. to 4*s*.

* * *

Moreover, as the period of inquiry approaches, the agriculturists, with the view of evading a true estimate of the qualities of their lands, throw much land out of cultivation; they cease to grow the most profitable kind of crops; they allow wells and water-courses to deteriorate, and the like. Such practices are equally, perhaps more, damaging to themselves than to the State; but they tend to keep back the improvement of the country.

Extracts from a Despatch from the Secretary of State to the Government of India, dated the 9th July, 1862.

That this general improvement will be accelerated by a permanent settlement Her Majesty's Government cannot entertain any doubt. A ready and popular mode of investment for the increasing wealth of the country will be provided by the creation of property in land, and all classes will benefit by the measure. On the agricultural population, the effect will be, as pointed out by Col. Baird Smith . . . . the elevation of the social condition of the people, and their consequent ability, not only to meet successfully the pressure occasioned by seasons of distress, but in ordinary times, to bear increased taxation in other forms without difficulty; the feeling of ownership, or, in other words, the absolute certainty of the full enjoyment of the reward for all the labour and capital which they may invest in the land will be sure to call out all their energies for its improvement. Her Majesty's Government confidently expect that a people in a state of contentment and progressive improvement will be able, without difficulty, to contribute to the revenue in other ways to such an extent as more than to compensate for the disadvantages of foregoing some prospective increase of that from land.

* * *

The course of events which has been anticipated is, indeed, only that which has taken place in every civilised country. Experience shows that in their early stages nations derived almost the whole of their public resources in a direct manner from the produce of the soil; but as they grew in wealth and civilisation, the basis of taxation has been changed, and the revenue has been in a great degree derived indirectly by means of imposts on articles which the increasing means of the people, consequent on a state of security and prosperity, have enabled them to consume in greater abundance. I am aware that it has been stated as an objection to promoting such a course of things in India, that in most European countries the advantages of this change have been mainly appropriated by the large landowners; but it must be remembered that in India, and specially in the districts under the ryotwari settlement, the great bulk of the agricultural population are the proprietors, subject only to the payment of the assessment, of the land which they till; and that, consequently, the benefit of a permanent settlement would be enjoyed, not by a narrow and limited class, but by the majority of the people.

APPENDIX B.

Statistics of the Famine of 1896-97.

	Area returned as distressed (sq. miles).	Population of distressed area (in thousands).	Maximum number on relief (in thousands).	Total units relieved (in thousands).	Average daily number on relief (in thousands).	Percentage of maximum number on relief to population.	Ratio of total units relieved to population.	Percentage of average number on relief to population.	Average cost of relief per 1,000 units relieved.
							Times.		Rs.
Madras	17,900	3,238	807	92,500	349	25	28	10	105
Bombay	42,000	6,710	454	114,000	358	7	17	5·3	106
Bengal	23,600	10,792	833	138,500	500	8	12	4·6	82
United Provinces	33,000	12,753	1,650	284,000	950	13	22	7·4	70
Central Provinces	50,000	6,168	698	138,000	479	11	22	7·7	99

APPENDIX C.

Extracts from the speech of the Hon. Mr. C. P. Ilbert introducing the Bengal Tenancy Bill into the Governor-General's Council.

If we trace it (this measure) to its ultimate origin we shall find that it embodies an endeavour to redeem a pledge which was given at the time of the Permanent Settlement, and which has never been adequately redeemed. If we examine its immediate causes, it will be easy to show that, for the last 20 years, there has been a persistent demand for a revision of the existing law, not merely on points of detail, but on points of principle; not merely as to procedure, but as to substantive rights; that this demand has grown in urgency with each succeeding year; that the subject has occupied the attention of success ve Lieut.-Governors of Bengal; that attempts have, at various times, been made to dispose of it by legislation in the Bengal Legislative Council; and that each unsuccessful attempt has shown the futility of any settlement which should deal only with procedure, and should leave the substantive rights of landlord and tenant untouched. What, then, are the facts with which we have to deal, and what are the evils for which legislation is required? Broadly stated, they are these. We have a population of some 60 millions mainly deriving their means of subsistence di ectly or indirectly from the soil; the great majority, directly, as cultivators; a small minority, indirectly, as rent-receivers. The mutual rights of these two classes, the rent-receivers and cultivators, are uncertain and obscure; the machinery for ascertaining and enforcing those rights is insufficient and defective; and the result is friction, which has taken different forms in different parts of the province. In Bihar, where the landlords are strong and the tenants are weak, we have rack-renting and acts of lawless and high-handed oppression on the part o the landlords; in Eastern Bengal where, comparatively speaking, the landlords are weak and th tenants strong, we have combinations of the tenants to resist the payment of rent. This is what Sir Ashley Eden said a few years ago of Bihar in a letter which he wrote as Lieut.-Governor, pointing out the urgent necessity for some reform in the law.

"In Bihar what is most wanted is some ready means of enabling he ryot to resist illegal distraint, illegal enhancement, and illegal cesses, and to prove and maintain his occupancy rights. Apart from the backwardness and poverty of the ryot, there are many points in the existing system of zemindari management in Bihar which seem to call for speedy amendment. The loose system of zemindari accounts, the entire absence of leases and counterparts, the universal prevalence of illegal distraint, the oppression incident to the realisation of rents in kind, the practice of amalgamating holdings so as to destroy evidence of continuous holding, are evils which necessarily prevent any possible development of agricultural prosperity among the tenant class, and place them practically at the mercy of their landlords or of the lessees, to whom, ordinarily, their landlords from time to time transfer their rights."

I said just now that the ultimate origin of the present measure might be traced back to the time of the Permanent Settlement. At that time, as now, there were three main classes interested in the soil of Bengal—the State, the revenue-payers or zemindars, and the cultivators or ryots. I am omitting, for the sake of simplicity, the persons holding intermediate interests between the zemindar and the ryot. Much learning has been devoted to ascertaining the precise position and rights of the zemindars and ryots at the time of the Permanent Settlement; but amidst the controversies which have for the last century raged, and are still raging on this subject, one point may be taken as conclusively proved, namely, that the great mass of the Bengal ryots were, at the time of the Permanent Settlement, in the enjoyment of certain customary rights which, at least, included the right of occupying the land conditionally on the payment of the rate of rent current and established in the locality, and I may add, the right of having that rate of rent determined by the State. Now, what the authors of the Permanent Settlement did was this: They settled and defined the mutual rights of the State and the revenue-payers or zemindars. They did not settle, define, or ascertain, the mutual rights of the zemindars and the ryots. They settled and defined the mutual rights of the State and the zemindars by declaring that the amount of revenue payable by the latter, which had formerly been fluctuating, or fixed for short terms of years, should be fixed for all time, and should not be increased by reason of any increase in the area under cultivation. And, at the same time, as part of the same settlement, they formally declared that the zemindars should be deemed to be the proprietors of the soil whatever that expression might mean; in other words, . . . they transferred to the zemindars those indefinite proprietary rights in the soil which had formerly been claimed by the State. But they did not settle or define, they did not even ascertain, the rights of the ryots or occupying cultivators. The legislation of 1793 left those rights outstanding and undefined, and by so leaving them, it tended to obscure them, to efface them, and, in too many cases, ultimately to destroy them. That both the Court of Directors in England, and the Governor-General in Council here, were aware of the possible consequences of their legislation, we well know. Immediately before the Permanent Settlement was made, the Court of Directors, in conveying instructions to the Government here, with respect to it, wrote as follows :—

"In order to leave no room for our instructions being at any time misunderstood, we direct you to be accurate in the terms in which our determination is announced . . . . You will, in a particular manner, be cautions so to express yourselves as to leave no ambiguity as to our right to interfere, from time to time, as it may be necessary, for the protection of the ryots and subordinate landlords, it being our intention, in the whole of this measure, effectually to limit our own demand, but not to depart from our inherent right, as Sovereigns, of being the guardians and protectors of every class of persons living under our Government."

Extract from a leading article in the "Statesman," dated 19th March, 1902.

Then came the most disastrous portion of his (Sir R. Temple's) career—disastrous, that is, to the people of this country. Early in January, 1874, he was appointed to superintend the relief operations in the famine-stricken districts of Bengal. Lord Northbrook, who was Viceroy at that time, was guided by the humane principle that the saving of life should be the first object of a British Government armed with absolute power, and therefore responsible for the lives of its helpless subjects. Up to that time the stereotyped official view had been that it was not the business of the Government to save the people alive in time of famine; that it was Utopian to attempt to do so, and that, in fact, so far from the State being called upon to combat the calamity, famine was a sort of God-send to clear off the surplus population. Lord Northbrook, to his lasting honour, was the first Viceroy of India to repudiate this abominable theory, and to recognise to the full the obligation of the State to do its utmost to keep the people alive in time of famine. But, unfortunately, he had, for his lieutenant, in

1874, Sir Richard Temple, who, readily adapting himself to the views then in the ascendant, proceeded to travesty the Viceroy's policy by instituting relief measures of such wasteful extravagance as to cover it with ridicule. Without taking the trouble to satisfy himself as to the true extent of the calamity—which as a matter of fact proved itself to be little more than temporary, though at the time severe, scarcity—he chartered ships by the dozen to bring rice from Burma and distant Saigon, and the Hooghly was filled with vessels laden with cargoes of grain amounting, in the aggregate, to 600,000 tons with which the authorities were quite unable to deal.

APPENDIX D.

Extracts from Appendices to the Famine Commission's Report of 1880, *regarding the influence of forests on rainfall and subsoil moisture.*

The disastrous effects of a general destruction of forests, on agriculture and pasturage, are generally known, and have been abundantly illustrated during the present century in south-eastern France; but it is still a question whether the total rainfall of a country is thereby diminished. Direct observations on the rainfall of forest-clad countries, large areas of which have subsequently been denuded, are unfortunately wanting; and it is perhaps open to question whether comparative rainfall measurements made in the forest and clearings of temperate countries which are still in large part covered with forests, and the clearings of which are either pasture land or under field cultivation, afford a criterion of the probable effects of a general denudation of forests in tropical and sub-tropical lands. A very elaborate series of comparative observations of the above kind, carried on for five years at eight pairs of stations in the forest and clearings of Bavaria by Dr. Ebermeyer, have led him to the conclusion that "in plains of uniform character the influence of forests on the quantity of rainfall is certainly very small. With increased elevation above the sea-level, the influence of forests becomes more important, and it has, therefore, a greater value in mountain tracts than on plains. In summer the effects of the forests is much greater than in winter. In the cold season it is evanescent. In warm southern countries it is greater than in cold countries; and in the interior of continents, where the humidity of the air and the annual precipitation are diminished, and the summer heat is greater, it plays a more important part than in the neighbourhood of coasts. From what has been said above, the clearing of a large area of country—at least of plain country—produces no essential diminution of the yearly rainfall. In hill tracts, on the contrary, after denudation there will be, on the whole, less rain than before. In all cases the destruction of forests will affect the rainfall only in the warm season, *i.e.*, during the summer months."

From the above it may be inferred that in a country such as India the consequences of a general destruction of forests would be more important than in Europe, since the climate of India is essentially continental, and over a large part of its area the temperature, even of the cool season, is not very far short of the average summer temperature of the countries of which Dr. Ebermeyer writes . . . . Judging from the known effects of forests upon climates, more specially of the temperature and humidity of the ground and lower strata of the air in contact with the ground, I should anticipate that the effect of extensive denudation would be to render storms more violent and spasmodic in character, and perhaps to diminish the frequency of gentle and continued rainfall.

* * *

The facts then adduced seemed to justify the conclusion that the foliage of trees greatly influence the purity, the humidity, and temperature of the atmosphere, and the supply of water on the earth's surface, by attracting clouds and condensing the moisture in the atmosphere, diminishing local temperature, protecting the soil from the action of the sun's rays, and husbanding the rain by regulating its flow.

In 1863, Mr. N. A. Dalzell, Conservator of Forests in the Bombay Presidency, ... showed that the wanton destruction of forests had entailed barrenness and aridity on countries renowned in former times for their fertility; that along with the woods, springs and rivulets disappear and cease to water the parched land; that the actual temperature of the country is, by the destruction of its forests, very sensibly increased; that the rain, gradually washing away the vegetable earth from the sides of the denuded hills, condemns them to sterility, while these latter, no longer able to retain and regulate the flow of water that falls on their slopes, are scored by deep gullies, formed by impetuous torrents, and the beds of rivers are at one time dry and at another filled by sudden and shortlived floods.

Mr. Robertson, the Superintendent of the Government Farms at Madras, ... found that during the last 30 years a large area of land had been denuded of trees, partly in view of an extension of arable culture, and partly to provide fuel for the railways and for domestic use. Seven hundred thousand acres, which were growing jungle scrub and coarse grass, had, during the preceding

18 years, been brought under the plough ; and, being now bare for two-thirds of the year, this must affect climate. The people unanimously declared that the rainfall had been gradually diminishing during the last 20 or 25 years, though it was not always referred to this cause.

Writing as to the future of the Peninsula (Madras), he (Sir Richard Temple) says : " . . . . . The southern peninsula of India has been, or is being, denuded not only of its forests, but also of its jungle, its groves, its brushwood, its trees. The denudation has been, I understand, going on near the sources and in the upper courses of the many rivers which water the country . . . . If it were to proceed unchecked there would be imminent danger of the rivers running dry by reason of the catchment basins and the drainage areas near their sources being rainless . . . . The progress of the country causes the price of timber and firewood to rise. The introduction of railways has, in the absence of any coal mines, greatly augmented the demand for fuel. Strong temptations are thus inevitably offered to the people at large to fell, cut, and lop recklessly, to bring every log, stump and stick to the market, to dig out the very roots of the jungle, so stopping any chance of reproduction, without thought for the future . . . . Any thoughtful spectator must perceive that, according to all meteorological experience, and to the almost certain teaching of proved facts, these fine distr cts were not destined by nature to be the prey and sport of famine and scarcity, but have been rendered subject to these calamities by the thoughtless action of man."

Ebermeyer has deduced the following result from his meteorological observations : "If from the soil of an open space, 100 parts of water evaporate, then from the soil of a forest tree from underwood 38 parts would evaporate, and from a soil covered with brushwood only 15 parts would evaporate. This simple fact explains clearly why the cutting down of wood over tracts of country is always followed by the drying up of wells and springs."

Extract from a report on the U.S. Bureau of Forestry.

In the San Bernardino mountains, records of precipitation for several years at a large number of stations show that differences in forest cover are closely correlated with differences in rainfall. This correlation is so close that it is possible to judge the mean annual precipitation with a fair degree of accuracy from the appearance of the forest alone. In these mountains, forests cover the slopes wherever the mean annual rainfall exceeds 20 to 24 inches; however, on southern and western slopes forests of equal density represent a larger rainfall than on northern or eastern slopes.

That the excessive destruction of forests is followed by the drying-up of streams and springs, and by a diminution in the minimum flow of rivers, is a well established fact. The forest is the most effective agent known in regulating the disposition of the precipitation after it reaches the ground.

Extract from a report by Mr. D. Howitz on the re-afforestation of waste lands in Ireland. (Parliamentary Return No. 39 *of* 1884.)

There can no longer be any doubt that the forests on ranges prevent sudden floods to a very great extent and that by a judicious cultivation of slopes and high plateaux in a few years these calamities are avoided. Experience has also proved that cultivations ensure a steady flow of water during summer, and that the fertility of the agricultural low lands is considerably increased by them. Baron Von Mueller, the celebrated botanist, states that in forest-bare coun'ries the productiveness of cereal fields increased 50 per cent. by the cultivation of forest belts—a statement never yet contradicted by experience. The work of re-afforesting will not only be a boon to the country at large by preventing the flooding of the low lands during heavy rains and fertilising them by a steady flow of water throughout the year, but it will have the great advantage of being a work eminently remunerative. That the planting of trees of even inferior quality will repay the trouble and thereby improve comparatively valueless land, you will grant when I refer you to the cultivation of *Les Landes* in France. Those localities, although so widely different from Ireland, are still a proof of what forest plantations can do. The Committee, which reported in 1857 on this work, predicted that the cultivation of the *Landes*, the low-lying lands near the Garonne, would add more than 1,000 million francs to the wealth of France—a prophecy which at that time was regarded as wild and foolish, but which has been more than fulfilled.

Extracts from the Evidence before the Select Committee on Forestry. (*Parliamentary Paper* 287 *of* 1885.)

[Evidence of Mr. Pedder, Secretary, Revenue Department, India Office.]

1. Yes, the destruction of forests was undoubtedly seriously affecting the water-supply in many parts of the country and seriously affecting the climate.

2. There are, no doubt, many instances in which it has been strongly suspected that the diminution of the water-supply of the streams has been caused by the cutting down of forests.

3. I ought to say that there is a great deal of evidence in India which tends to show that the denudation process has had an effect upon the water-supply in two ways: one in diminishing the moisture of the country in the way of falls of rain, and another in making the rain run away more rapidly, and causing floods.

4. In the north of the Punjab it has been represented by men, whose opinions are of great weight, that the denudation of some of the Himalayan forests has caused great destruction from the way in which the torrents have washed immense masses of sand and stone from the mountains into the plain.

5. *Q.*—And is it not well recognised that the growth of forests leads to the storage of water and its gradually being distributed in streamlets and rivulets to the streams which it ultimately supplies.

A.—I believe that is an unquestionable fact, and is the foundation of all forestry.

6. There is a district called Ratnagiri, south of Bombay; it is a rice district, which lies between the sea and the Western Ghats, which used to be considered to be the most productive of the rice lands of the west of India at that time—I am speaking of 50 years ago—and I know from the reports I have read of the officers who were employed to make the original trigonometrical survey that that country was covered by dense forests. The diaries of those officers show that in some cases they had to cut a base line at the rate of half a mile a day for miles through dense forest, whereas now the same district has been entirely denuded up to the crest of the hills. The hills are almost a bare sheet of rock, and people have complained, and complained bitterly, of the decreasing yield of the rice land below, which has been attributed, and I believe truly, to the destruction of the forests, which operates, of course, to prevent the water from being stored upon the hill sides; it runs away in violent floods instead of flowing gently over the country.

[Evidence of Col. James Michael, C.S.I.]

1. *Q.*—What is your opinion of the influence of the denudation of forests upon the rainfall and water-supply as derived from original observations ?

A.—I personally have no doubt whatever upon the subject; in fact, I have seen myself the effects of the denudation of hill slopes. I have seen a well known perennial stream dried up completely upon the slopes of the Nilgiris undoubtedly from the fact that the timber all round it had been cut off for coffee planting.

2. *Q.*—Was that a stream which had been perennial ?

A.—Yes, it had been perennial, and it had utterly dried up. I have seen several at the station of Ootacamund ; I can quote a particular spring near the church of Ootacamund which used to be always the source from which most people got their drinking water ; it was an excellent spring, and within my memory the wood which surrounded that spring was cut down, the result being that the spring has disappeared, and that there is no water there now.

I can mention many instances of springs being lost from a forest being cut away, but not of any spring being formed by the formation of a forest ; though I have no doubt that would be the case in years to come.

APPENDIX E.

The two severe famines through which the Central Provinces have passed during the last few years have had a direct and serious effect upon the condition of education, as is shown in the quinquennial Report just published. School attendance was reduced, and the funds available for education were curtailed. The end of the period, however, was marked by a return to a happier state of things, and progress is now fairly satisfactory. The most interesting part of the Report, and the part which records the most noteworthy improvement, is that dealing with the revision of primary school instruction, and the attempts to give it a more practical bent. The bulk of the population is agricultural, and under the revised scheme elementary instruction in agriculture has been given a prominent place. *A very sensible move was made by dropping agriculture as a special subject*, and making it a part of the ordinary reading lesson. The text-book on agriculture was embodied in the vernacular reading books, and a revision of the curriculum was made for the special benefit of agriculturists, who were required to attend school for three hours in the morning so as to admit of their spending the rest of the day in their ordinary occupations. Such pupils were classed as half-timers. For whole-timers the curriculum involved a more extensive course, and was designed for those boys who wished to continue their studies beyond the Upper Primary stage. Among the subjects introduced with an eye to their practical usefulness for the sons of agriculturists, were the elements of the law of landlord and tenant, the portion of the text-book bearing on the subject being incorporated with the ordinary reading books. Instruction in patwaris' papers and mahajani accounts is also being given. Every boy is now required to understand and to write in his own hand village revenue papers, and the patwari is appointed a member of the School Committee, with a view of assisting the master in explaining these papers to the boys. In the case of some schools the patwari accompanies the boys into the fields and explains to them the nature of the crops and soils. Every primary school is provided with a copy of the patwari's village map, and every boy is required to understand it and to draw a copy of it himself. School gardens, some of them well stocked with European and Indian vegetables, exist in most primary schools, as a means of providing occupation and instruction for the boys. "Our course of instruction," says the Report, " may in fact be said to carry out what Sir E. Buck has described as the proper method of education for the cultivating classes, *viz.*, 'the lowest form of literary education compatible with such training of the faculties as will enable them to grasp the meaning of the agricul ural experiments offered them and to protect themselves against their natural enemies— the landlord, the money-lender, and the Government official.'"

APPENDIX F.

Principal Subjects of Technical Instruction.

1. Agricultural science.
2. Dairy work.
3. Poultry-keeping.
4. Sheep-shearing.
5. Ploughing.
6. Forestry.
7. Fruit culture.
8. Milking.
9. Management of live-stock.
10. Stacking and thatching.
11. Pisci-culture.
12. Veterinary science.
13. Plaiting.
14. Horticulture and gardening.
15. Bee-keeping.
16. Carpentry and joinery.
17. Wood-carving.
18. Carriage building.
19. Pattern-making.
20. Basket-making.
21. Cardboard work.
22. Modelling in clay and wood.
23. Sail-making.
24. Lithography and book-binding.
25. Photography.
26. Plumbing.
27. Plastering.
28. Masonry and brickwork.
29. Painting and decorating.
30. Forged iron work.
31. Cookery.
32. Laundry.
33. Domestic economy.
34. Manual instruction.
35. Land-draining.
36. Hat manufacture.
37. Paper-making.
38. Dress-making and millinery.
39. Needlework and embroidery.
40. Lace-making.
41. Shoe-making.
42. Farriery work.
43. Leather work.
44. Dyeing and bleaching.
45. Cotton-spinning and weaving.
46. Nursing and Ambulance work.

APPENDIX G.

Extract from a leading article in the "Times," of February 6, 1903.

There is no doubt that great and perhaps growing anxiety is felt in many quarters concerning the scarcity of our national food-supply in time of war. Certain facts bearing upon the question are indisputable. These islands now rely very largely on martime imports for their subsistence, and being islands, they must either grow the food they require on their own soil, or import it from over the seas. Some three-fourths of the food we consume is thus imported, and the great bulk of it is carried in British ships. These ships, and all other ships flying the British flag, are liable to capture or destruction at sea in time of war by an enemy who is strong enough to hold his own against the British Navy. If our food ran short, or if there were any serious danger of its running short, the price of food must rise throughout the country. There are several millions of the population who live already on the margin of subsistence, and these millions would, in the event of the price of food rising seriously, be brought within measurable distance of starvation, if not face to face with it. There are many more millions who are only able to maintain themselves, some in comparative comfort, and some in little more than penury, because they are able to earn sufficient wages to support them by employment in the production of the commodities which we export to pay for our food. The interruption, or even the serious constriction, of our imported food-supplies, would thus automatically entail a corresponding interruption or constriction of our internal industries, and would thereby add many millions to the ranks of the unemployed and the ill-nourished. What would be the effect of the discontent thus engendered by present want and impending starvation on the policy of the country in a life-and-death struggle with its enemies, no man can say exactly; but we all must feel that the situation would be a very alarming one.

APPENDIX H.

The extent of Great Britain's dependence on foreign countries for her food-supply may be judged from the fact that she consumes corn and grain exported by the United States of the value of 24 million pounds sterling; by Russia, of the value of 9½ millions; by Roumania, 7½ millions; by the Argentine Republic, 5 millions; and by Canada, 4½ millions. She depends for meat on foreign countries to the extent of 32½ millions, to which Denmark contributes 4, Australia 4, Holland 2½, and the United States 20 millions. Of the total dairy produce (*e.g.*, butter, cheese, eggs, etc.) of the value of 33½ millions which she imports from foreign countries, Denmark sends 11 millions, Holland 5½ millions, France 4 millions, and the United States 5 millions. These statistics show the extent of Great Britain's dependence for her food requirements, the total annual value of which exceeds 191 millions pounds sterling. From this figure some allowance has to be made for the articles used in manufactured products which are exported.